AI Applications in Business

The Silicon Valley playbook for AI is broken. It's time for a better way.

While tech giants race to deploy faster and bigger AI models, businesses worldwide are discovering that speed without strategy leads to expensive failures. The real winners aren't those who adopt AI first, but those who adopt it wisely.

This book offers a unique perspective on how ancient philosophies hold the key to AI success. From Chinese *wu wei* (effortless action) to Japanese *kaizen* (continuous improvement) to South African *ubuntu* (interconnectedness), time-tested wisdom offers powerful frameworks for navigating AI's promises and pitfalls.

Discover why:

- Ancient philosophies outperform Silicon Valley thinking
- Cultural wisdom beats venture capital hype
- Strategic patience trumps technological urgency
- Ethical deployment creates a lasting competitive advantage

Whether you're a CEO, manager, or entrepreneur, this book provides cultural in sights and practical frameworks you need to deploy AI thoughtfully, strategically, and successfully.

The future belongs not to those who move quickly, but to those who move wisely.

AF763805

"Drawing on decades of leadership experience, the author makes a compelling case that the winners in the AI era won't be those who adopt technology the fastest, but those who integrate it the most thoughtfully. With real-world insights and cross-cultural perspectives, this book is essential reading for business and technology leaders who want AI strategies that are practical, ethical, and sustainable—not just Silicon Valley hype."
Kelvin Looi, *Former Vice President, Data & AI, IBM*

"Vicki Liu delivers an impressive exploration of AI in business, offering a professional deep dive into diverse practices across industries. This book shows how AI can be applied in different countries and cultures, filled with vivid examples and global insights."
Selina Yuan, *SVP, Alibaba Cloud Intelligence Group*

"As a VP of Product Management in data management, I see this book as both a guide and a call to action. It captures the urgency of today's AI era—where trusted data, strong governance, and the rise of intelligent agents are redefining how organizations operate—while also providing a practical roadmap for leaders to move beyond pilots, scale responsibly, and build AI-first enterprises. For anyone navigating the convergence of data and AI, this book offers both inspiration and concrete strategies to shape the future of business transformation."
John Thomas, *VP of Product, Informatica*

"AI's greatest value lies not in efficiency gains but as a fundamental capability multiplier—transforming industries globally. This book is essential for leaders looking to understand and leverage AI's adaptive power across diverse markets in Asia, Africa, Latin America and beyond."
Xiaomei Wang, *Founder & CEO, PathoAI*

AI Applications in Business

Beyond Silicon Valley and Western Frameworks

Vicki Liu

CRC Press
Taylor & Francis Group
Boca Raton London New York

CRC Press is an imprint of the
Taylor & Francis Group, an **informa** business
A CHAPMAN & HALL BOOK

Designed cover image: Shutterstock ID: 1421446100

First edition published 2026
by CRC Press
2385 NW Executive Center Drive, Suite 320, Boca Raton FL 33431

and by CRC Press
4 Park Square, Milton Park, Abingdon, Oxon, OX14 4RN

CRC Press is an imprint of Taylor & Francis Group, LLC

ISBN: 9781041082897 (hbk)
ISBN: 9781041082880 (pbk)
ISBN: 9781003644699 (ebk)

DOI: 10.1201/9781003644699

Typeset in Minion
by KnowledgeWorks Global Ltd.

To my Ksenia, I wrote this for the world you will inherit. You are my motivation to make it better.

Contents

Preface

Two years ago, my father suddenly passed away. Without warning. I had just 11 days with him in the hospital. Eleven precious days to share everything that mattered. When he was gone, I felt like the ground had opened up beneath me, threatening to pull me into a darkness I couldn't escape.

As I painfully sorted through his belongings, I found myself searching for any words he had left behind—thoughts, notes, anything he had written down. I treasured every piece I could find. My father was a brilliant man: articulate, gifted with a remarkable memory, well-read, and full of wonderful insights. But I discovered he hadn't written much down systematically. I found myself wishing he had captured more of his wisdom on paper, not just for me, but for future generations who would never have the chance to know him.

That's when it hit me. I began thinking about my own children and what I might leave behind for them. What would they know about who I am, other than being their mom? What would they understand about my work, my passions, the way I see the world, and how I've tried to make a difference?

I want them to know the person behind the parent. I want them to know my life's work, the challenges I've dealt with, and the small ways I've tried to contribute to the world they'll inherit.

That's the heart of this book. It's my way of passing along not just knowledge, but the intention to leave tomorrow's generation a better world to build upon.

Introduction

Beyond Silicon Valley: Why Ancient Wisdom Holds the Key to AI's Future in Business

The biggest shifts in human history didn't happen because someone found a way to complete the same tasks faster. They happened because someone ventured beyond what was thought possible. When our ancestors began drawing symbols on cave walls, they weren't just doodling. They figured out how to store thoughts outside their own minds: they created the first external memory system which allowed humans to pass knowledge across generations. The printing press mattered not because it could make books (scribes had been copying books for centuries). It was revolutionary because it broke the Church's monopoly on information, sparking literacy and playing a crucial role in the Scientific Revolution. Alexander Graham Bell's telephone didn't just enable people to talk over long distances, it shattered the idea that real conversation required being in the same room. It changed business and personal relationships forever.

What these moments have in common is that, rather than simply improving existing processes, they made us reconsider fundamental assumptions about human capability, which is exactly what is happening with artificial intelligence today.

WHAT AI ACTUALLY IS

Stripping away the hype, AI is really just our effort to build systems that observe, understand, and learn, just like humans do. The big difference is that these systems can process information at lightning speed, making our existing methods pale in comparison.

What started off as mere academic curiosity has become the most significant technological shift any of us will witness in our lifetime. Since 2020, AI has gone from something to "keep an eye on" to an integral part of our everyday lives, actively transforming our world as we know it.

Companies are facing their biggest opportunity and most alarming threat simultaneously. AI promises to solve problems that have been plaguing us for decades and unlock productivity gains we never imagined. But it's also threatening to make entire business models obsolete overnight.

THE UNCOMFORTABLE TRUTH

Five years ago, executives would ask me, "will this AI stuff actually be relevant to my business?" Just last month, the CEO of a mid-sized manufacturing company pulled me aside at a conference and said, "my competitor just launched a predictive maintenance system that makes it look like we're using stone tools. How do I catch up before we are outpaced?"

The direction of our questions has changed. Most business executives now believe that AI is no longer optional for their business. It's becoming a fundamental requirement just to stay in the game.

The reality facing business leaders today is that they don't get to choose whether AI affects their business anymore. That choice has already been made for them. Companies that are unable to perform meaningful AI integration will be demolished by competitors who can process information faster, make better decisions, and adapt to changes more effectively.

I have watched seemingly untouchable companies get knocked sideways by startups that adopted AI ahead of the curve. These newcomers deliver customer experiences that feel remarkably personalized, enabling proactive service and tailored recommendations. Their operations run like clockwork, while established players are still stuck at the drawing board trying to figure out their next move.

In short, the winners aren't always the ones with the biggest budgets or the longest history. They are the ones who learn to use AI strategically, instead of slapping it on top of what they are already doing.

BEYOND SILICON VALLEY THINKING

Most AI business books follow the same script: Silicon Valley innovation culture mixed with American individualism and European management theory. It's all about moving fast, breaking things, and assuming that having better technology automatically gives companies a competitive edge.

That narrow view quickly falls apart in the real world, where different cultures, values, and the collective welfare of communities actually do matter.

I have seen the Silicon Valley playbook work brilliantly in Palo Alto and fail spectacularly in Mumbai, Jakarta, or São Paulo. While Silicon Valley builds the technology, the wisdom for using it sustainably and responsibly often come from philosophies that have been guiding civilizations for millennia.

Take *wu wei* from Chinese philosophy as an example: this concept of effortless action could revolutionize how humans and AI collaborate. Or Japan's *kaizen* approach involving continuous improvement, which transforms how you iterate AI systems. *Ubuntu* ("I am because we are") from South African ideology reframes AI ethics around community well-being instead of individual rights.

These aren't just alternative perspectives, but rather deliberate frameworks for solving AI's toughest challenges.

WHAT THIS BOOK DOES DIFFERENTLY

In this book, you will be taken through AI's evolution from being a lab experiment to becoming business reality. We will look at global use cases to determine what is working, what is failing, and what comes next across ten critical areas, ranging from understanding AI's disruptions and opportunities to transforming business models with AI.

We will do this by balancing innovation with shared responsibility, looking at leadership through different cultural perspectives, and exploring how various regions approach AI in ways that reflect their unique circumstances.

CALL TO ACTION

The companies that dominate the AI era won't be the ones that implement AI the quickest or with the most flash. It will be those that approach AI thoughtfully, by balancing competitive pressure with cultural insight, operational excellence with ethical responsibility, and ambitious goals with adaptive flexibility.

Success means moving past the primitive "adopt AI or die" mentality, and developing the sophisticated ability to deploy AI in ways that are effective but deeply principled.

This is about democratizing AI knowledge beyond its Western-centric bubble, thus giving business leaders everywhere more nuanced, sustainable, and effective strategies for AI integration—strategies that respect different approaches, cultural values, and ways of thinking to thrive in our rapidly evolving world.

About the Author

Vicki Liu is Chief Executive Officer of Apogem AI and a globally recognized expert in artificial intelligence. She has two decades of experience at the forefront of the AI revolution. As both a Fortune 500 advisor and startup mentor, she bridges the gap between cutting-edge AI innovation and practical business transformation.

Vicki's expertise spans advanced analytics, data management, digital transformation, and information governance. Her career trajectory reflects the evolution of AI itself, starting from the stage of early adoption to today's era of widespread transformation. She previously served as Vice President for IBM Asia-Pacific, and Vice President and General Manager at Mastech InfoTrellis, where she orchestrated large-scale AI initiatives that reshaped how organizations operate worldwide.

Her deep AI expertise was cultivated during her 15 years with IBM's consulting organization, where she led major artificial intelligence and digital transformation projects for Fortune 500 companies and government entities across North and South America, Europe, and the Asia-Pacific. Vicki began her technology career at 3M, spearheading e-commerce transformation initiatives. An accomplished educator and thought leader, Vicki combines technical depth with strategic vision. She holds an MBA from Colorado State University and a Master's degree in Computer Science from Western University.

Through her work, Vicki has become a trusted voice in how artificial intelligence will reshape industries, governments, and society. Her insights draw from real-world experience in implementing AI solutions at the highest level of global organizations, making her perspective both practical and visionary.

CHAPTER 1

The AI Revolution

Disruption, Opportunities, and Risks

SECTION 1: THE GENESIS OF ARTIFICIAL INTELLIGENCE

1.1 PHILOSOPHICAL FOUNDATIONS

The concept of artificial intelligence (AI) has roots that stretch back thousands of years into ancient human history. Myths and legends across cultures describe artificial beings granted the power of thought, from the golems of Jewish folklore to Talos, the bronze automaton of Greek mythology, to Pangu (盘古), the ancient Chinese mythological figure who structured chaos into order, which inspired modern Chinese AI development, including Huawei's Pangu AI Model.

The philosophical underpinnings of AI began to take more concrete form during the Enlightenment in Europe. Rene Descartes, in his 1637 work *Discourse on the Method*, proposed a dualistic view of existence that separated mind from matter.[1] This separation raised profound questions: if the mind is distinct from physical matter, could an artificial mind be created? Conversely, if thought is merely a physical process occurring in the brain, could it be replicated in another physical system?

By the 19th century, mathematicians were laying groundwork that would prove crucial for AI's development. George Boole's work on symbolic logic created a system where logical reasoning could be performed through algebraic manipulation—essentially turning reasoning into a form of calculation. Ada Lovelace, working with Charles Babbage on the analytical engine,

DOI: 10.1201/9781003644699-1

envisioned machines that could manipulate symbols to produce outputs that had not been explicitly programmed.[2] In her notes, she wrote,

> The Analytical Engine has no pretensions whatever to originate anything. It can do whatever we know how to order it to perform… But it is likely to exert an indirect influence on science itself in another manner. For, in distributing and combining the truths and the formulas of analysis, the relations and the nature of many subjects in that science are necessarily thrown into new lights, and more profoundly investigated.[3]

Ada's notes hinted at what we now see as one of AI's key characteristics: not just following a set of instructions but also being able to recognize patterns and connections within datasets that we may have overlooked, providing deeper insights in existing scenarios.

1.2 FROM THEORY TO REALITY: THE BIRTH OF AI AS A FIELD

The formal emergence of AI as a recognized field of study is generally traced to the Dartmouth Summer Research Project on AI, held in the summer of 1956. Organized by cognitive scientists and computer engineers widely considered to be the founding fathers of AI, the workshop proposed that "every aspect of learning […] can in principle be so precisely described that a machine can be made to simulate it."[4]

The workshop created a vision to build machines that could form ideas, solve problems like humans, and learn to continually improve themselves (see endnote 4). While the two-month endeavor didn't immediately achieve their target, it officially put AI on the map as a distinct and credible field of research.

After the Dartmouth Conference, AI pioneers began to make remarkable progress. The optimism of this early period was infectious. Simon and Newell famously predicted in 1958 that within ten years a digital computer would be the world's chess champion, as well as discover and prove a mathematical theorem.[5] While these predictions proved premature, they reflected the genuine excitement surrounding the field's potential.

1.3 THE AI WINTER AND SPRING CYCLES

AI's progress hasn't been a smooth journey. There have been countless breakthroughs and excitement surrounding the novel topic but also periods when enthusiasm has faded and funding dried up. These high and low periods are called the "AI winters and springs," a cycle the field has gone through several times over the years.

The first major setback came in the late 1960s. Researchers ran into problems they hadn't anticipated. For one, machine translation proved to be difficult when sentences were translated literally, ignoring nuances in both languages. They discovered that understanding language wasn't just about word-for-word transcription; it required a deep understanding of context clues to overcome obstacles such as word ambiguity, differing sentence structures, and idioms. They began to realize that language was something that could not be taught through textbooks alone but required real-world experience to master—but how could this be achieved through a machine? By 1973, the Lighthill Report in the United Kingdom severely criticized AI's failure to achieve its overzealous goals, leading to reduced government funding in both Britain and the United States.[6]

AI made a big comeback in the 1980s, largely thanks to expert systems—programs built to mimic how human experts made decisions in specific fields. Having shown great promise, companies invested heavily in the technology. By 1985, the global market for AI reached $1 billion.[7] However, these systems were expensive to maintain and ultimately didn't deliver on their commercial promises. The excitement quickly faded, leading to yet another famous "winter."

But every AI winter eventually has to pass. Even when the hype faded, AI researchers kept hope, continuing to test new ideas, optimize algorithms, and drive breakthroughs from a limited pool of data, waiting for the world to catch up. And what emerges isn't just a recurrence but a renaissance.

SECTION 2: THE MODERN AI RENAISSANCE: KEY TECHNOLOGICAL BREAKTHROUGHS

2.1 THE RISE OF MACHINE LEARNING

The modern AI boom really took off in the late 1990s and early 2000s, when researchers started rethinking their entire approach. Instead of trying to hand-code every rule for intelligent behavior—a method that dominated early AI—they shifted their focus to building systems that could actually learn from data.[8]

This idea wasn't entirely new. Back in the 1950s, pioneers like Arthur Samuel were already experimenting with learning algorithms, like a checkers program built to learn from itself while playing.[9] Neural networks in the 1980s, inspired by how the human brain works, had also shown some promise. Unfortunately, computers just weren't powerful enough, and there weren't sufficient training data back then to make the system practical.[10] What really changed the game in the modern era were three big things:

- **Computer pricing:** Computers got a lot faster and cheaper thanks to Moore's Law, making complex algorithms possible.
- **Data generation:** We began generating mountains of data from the internet, smartphones, and digital businesses, giving machine learning systems the raw material they needed.
- **Algorithm breakthroughs:** Researchers made major breakthroughs in algorithms, coming up with smarter ways to help machines learn, including revisiting ideas that were previously unsuccessful. This led to systems like AlphaGo that managed to defeat world champions in the board game Go.[11]

By the early 2000s, machine learning was being put to practical use. Companies like Amazon and Google began to use it for product recommendations or to improve search results. This shift was huge, as these systems were able to draw conclusions from external stimuli and information on their own, learning from experience much like people do.

2.2 DEEP LEARNING: THE GAME CHANGER

If machine learning was a big shift in AI, then deep learning was a revolution within that revolution. This approach uses multiple layers of artificial neural networks to analyze information, mimicking the way the human brain works. It was designed to process huge amounts of raw data and automatically discern important features that would have been almost impossible for humans to identify manually.

The breakthrough moment for deep learning happened in 2012 at the ImageNet Large Scale Visual Recognition Challenge, an annual competition where software programs compete to correctly identify objects in images. A deep neural network called AlexNet won the challenge. It absolutely crushed the competition by greatly reducing the error rate for image recognition and made a revolutionary leap that caught the attention of the entire AI community[12].

What AlexNet achieved sparked an explosion of interest and investment in deep learning. Companies rushed to acquire talent and startups in the space. Google acquired DeepMind for over $500 million in 2014.[13]

Facebook, Microsoft, Amazon, and other tech giants all set up dedicated AI research labs led by scholars who pioneered in the field.

The benefits of deep learning were quickly recognized in multiple fields, including computer vision, speech recognition, and natural language processing. Its ability to process raw data directly helped reduce the need for feature engineering, the labor-intensive process where relevant aspects of data must be specified for machine learning models. Deep neural networks could discover useful features automatically, often finding patterns that humans overlooked.

2.3 THE HARDWARE REVOLUTION: GPUs AND TPUs

The deep learning revolution wouldn't have been possible without the breakthroughs in hardware. Traditional Central Processing Units (CPUs) were good for sequential processing but not efficient for the massive computing power required by neural networks.

Graphics Processing Units (GPUs), which were first built to power video game graphics, turned out to be perfect for training neural networks. NVIDIA immediately recognized this opportunity and repositioned their GPUs for AI applications. The company released CUDA, a platform allowing developers to use GPUs for general computing tasks.

GPUs completely changed the game. What used to take weeks on CPUs could now be done in just days or even hours. Researchers could test new ideas more quickly and train models on far bigger datasets than before.

As AI workloads continued to grow, technology companies started to develop custom AI chips for specific types of tasks. Google introduced Tensor Processing Units (TPUs), integrated circuits designed explicitly for accelerating deep learning.[14] Amazon, Facebook, and others followed with their own specialized AI hardware.

This new hardware development kicked off a snowball effect. Better chips created smarter AI modes which led to more breakthroughs that brought more talent and funding into the field. All that investment then went right back into developing even more powerful hardware, and the cycle kept accelerating.

2.4 BIG DATA: THE FUEL FOR MODERN AI

Algorithms are like the engine of AI, hardware gives it horsepower, and data is the fuel that it all runs on. The exponential growth in digital data, generated through increased internet activity and mobile device usage, has provided continuous streams of location, usage, and sensor statistics. As companies began moving operations online, more business data became usable through this digitization process. Connected devices, from industrial equipment to consumer appliances, began continuously reporting operational data, and cheaper storage made it economically feasible to store and process massive datasets.

This vast amount of data made today's AI systems possible. Modern language models train on hundreds of billions of words from reading books, articles, and websites.[15] Computer vision systems learn from millions of labeled images. Recommendation systems analyze billions of user interactions.

The correlation between data availability and AI performance is clear. In many applications, models with more complete data outperformed more sophisticated algorithms trained on less data. As Google's research director Peter Norvig famously stated, "We don't have better algorithms. We just have more data."[16]

2.5 FROM NARROW TO GENERAL INTELLIGENCE: THE SPECTRUM OF AI CAPABILITIES

Most of the AI applications we come across every day, from spam filters, grammar checkers, or movie recommendations on streaming services, is what we call "narrow" or "weak" AI. These systems are incredibly good at the specific tasks they were built and trained for. For example, a chess AI bot can beat the best players in the world, but it can't teach a beginner to play or explain the origin of the gambits it uses. These AI models are amazing specialists, but they lack the common sense, flexibility, and broad thinking necessary for applying their knowledge to more general use cases.

With the advancement in software, hardware, and abundance of data, we are seeing AI systems that have started to grow general abilities to perform broader functions. Take transfer learning for example: here, you can train a model to detect tumors, then adapt the same model to detect anomalies in retinal scans,[17] just like the human ability to distinguish cats from dogs. Then come few-shot and zero-shot learning, which allow a model to perform tasks with very few or sometimes no prior training examples.[18] These systems have started to develop the human ability of understanding how to solve a problem without preexisting knowledge. We are also seeing multi-model learning, a key technology involved in autonomous vehicle development, where multiple sources (text, images, audio, etc.) are used to train AI models to improve performance. While AI systems are still struggling with using the five senses simultaneously, they are getting closer to achieving how we process the information around us naturally.

All of this progress has people talking about AGI (artificial general intelligence) again, which is AI that can think and solve problems as humans do. Most experts still think we are nowhere near that point, but the line between "narrow" and "general" AI is getting increasingly more blurred as time goes on. Researchers cannot agree on when or even if AGI can be achieved. Some say a few decades, others think it could take centuries, and some aren't sure if it's possible at all. We have made incredible progress with AI problem-solving that nobody believed possible just decades ago. However, human intelligence has proved to be far more difficult to replicate than we initially thought. The truth is, we are still trying to figure out how our own minds work, so predicting when we will build equivalent artificial ones is not an easy call to make.

SECTION 3: THE TRANSFORMATIONAL IMPACT OF AI IN THE BUSINESS WORLD

Nowadays, we seem to expect and often welcome AI's involvement in our work, education, and leisure. Based on repeated habits at specific times of day, smart appliances adjust at-home lighting and temperature automatically. On the way to work, your GPS reroutes in real time to avoid traffic jams. In the office, your emails are sorted into "Promotions," "Social," and "Updates" tabs to save time. According to McKinsey's 2025 report regarding AI in the workplace,[19] companies from small businesses to global enterprises are starting to recognize that AI is opening countless doors to help serve customers more personally and work more efficiently, enabling them to reimagine future possibilities for their business.

The companies that do well in this changing world are not always the most substantial. They're the ones who are willing and ready to use technology to address real business problems for the customers they serve. Think about it: AI can process huge amounts of data in minutes, automate tedious routine tasks, and discover hidden insights that human eyes may fail to notice. Traditional barriers to entry are quickly dissolving as AI technologies become more readily available. Corporations are realizing that they can ditch the old rulebook and find entirely new ways to create value for their customers, competing in a way that their competitors can't easily replicate.

More specifically, AI is reshaping competition itself. Rather than competing in the traditional way on cost or product innovation, companies

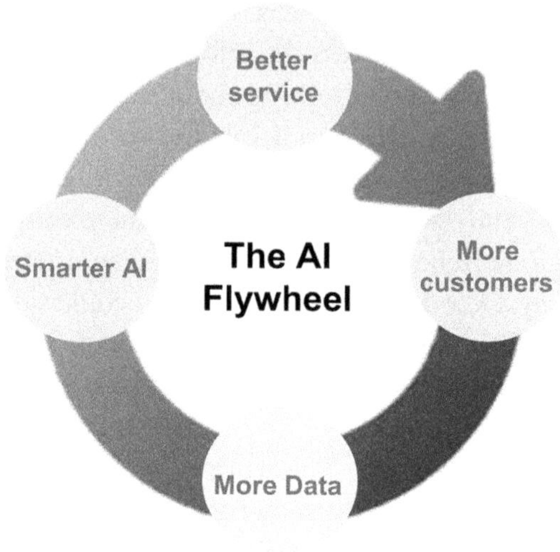

FIGURE 1.1 The AI flywheel.

are now challenging how well they can leverage AI to learn faster, adapt quicker, and deliver exactly what each customer wants before they even realize that they want it. This creates a powerful AI flywheel (see Figure 1.1), a self-reinforcing cycle where gaining more customers generates more data, which improves AI intelligence, leading to better services that attract even more customers.

Let's take a look at some examples of how AI is driving these changes in real-world business scenarios.

3.1 UNLOCKING NEW REVENUE STREAMS AND MARKETS

AI is great at spotting patterns in huge amounts of data, uncovering opportunities that would have otherwise gone unnoticed. This goes for tapping into a new market, or addressing customer needs that haven't yet been met. For example,

- **Predictive analytics**: This is being used across various industries, commonly in healthcare, human resources, and supply chain. Retailers like Amazon and Alibaba use AI to stay a step ahead of what customers want so they can stock the right products and avoid waste of resources. Alibaba's AI platform, ET Brain, also analyzes historical sales data, weather patterns, holidays, and social trends to predict future demand.[20] All these technical capabilities help them optimize inventory, create "You May Also Like" lists, and drive sales, which is especially critical ahead of peak shopping seasons like Singles' Day. The holiday, originating in 2009 as a celebration for those without partners, has now grown into a massive online shopping extravaganza held every year on November 11th, chosen for the symbolism of the four solitary "1"s. Alibaba records a Gross Merchandise Value (GMV) of over $84 billion US during the Singles' Day sales period in 2021,[21] which grew from a humble $7 million US in 2009. They were able to achieve almost 10× the US online Black Friday sales that year.[22]

Another interesting use case is in human resources. Alibaba also uses predictive analytics extensively in its HR operations for hiring and retention, as well as general HR functions such as performance and resource management. These solutions can greatly reduce operational costs, especially when the labor market is volatile.

- **Niche market identification:** Both startups and tech giants in Asia are using AI to discover micro trends early, or to find customer segments that have been underserved traditionally. Pinduoduo, in China, has one of the most remarkable startup stories I've come across. While e-commerce giants were chasing big-city shoppers, Pinduoduo noticed that there was a huge untapped market in smaller cities where people wanted to buy in bulk, simultaneously trying to be price-conscious.[23] Their AI analyzed search queries and purchasing patterns in lower-tier cities (Tiers 3–5) and identified price-sensitive, bulk-buying trends—and immediately took action. In 2024, nine years after inception, Pinduoduo's annual revenue reached $54 billion US,[24] a mind-blowing 59% growth rate year after year for five straight years.

  Then there is Zomato, in India, which started as any other restaurant review site. It has since grown into something much bigger with the help of AI. They realized their real advantage was in the data they had. AI analyzed what people searched for, as well as patterns in their restaurant reviews,[25] and discovered several local food trends that nobody else was keeping track of. Suddenly, they could tell you that people in Delhi were going crazy for Chettinad food or that Bangalore was obsessed with Japanese desserts. That insight helped them evolve from a simple review platform into a major digital service company that became a cornerstone for pinpointing new trends through truly understanding local tastes.

3.2 HUMAN–AI CO-CREATION

AI is becoming our new creative partner across various industries. Beyond automation, it's helping artists, designers, and marketers generate new ideas, overcoming creative blocks, and exploring fresh directions altogether.

By learning from massive datasets such as artistic styles, design patterns, and market trends, AI can suggest unexpected combinations like patterns and offer new starting points for creative work. This shift is changing our perception of creativity itself. Instead of man *or* machine, it's becoming man *plus* machine. And this is just the beginning; below are a couple examples of how this trend is unfolding in the real world:

- **AI-native workforce models and co-creation with generative AI:** A new kind of workforce is emerging, dubbed "AI-native." This group of people works with AI seamlessly in their daily routines. This can exist in any job function, regardless of whether they have technical background or not. This shift is super clear with generative AI, where humans and AI bots team up to create text, images, video, code, or designs.[26] In this working relationship, AI helps brainstorm ideas while human experts verify its output, ensuring alignment with their long-term vision and verifying that ethical considerations are met. The result is a powerful partnership stretching far beyond just efficiency. By combining human judgment with AI's speed and power, we can make smarter decisions and drive faster innovation.
- **Dynamic content creation and live shopping:** Gojek, Indonesia's go-to app for ride-hailing and food delivery, utilizes dynamic bundling and is a prime example of us working together with AI to solidify brand loyalty. Gojek's AI technique uses graph neural networks to map the relationship between services (such as ride-hailing, food delivery, and payments) and offer real-time deals.[27] For example, if a user orders nasi goreng via GoFood at 9 PM, it suggests a discounted GoCar ride home. It also factors in rainfall data to offer instant "rain-safe" bundle deals when it pours in Jakarta. Through these offerings, Gojek achieves significantly higher average order value for users accepting AI bundles. Another example of dynamic content creation is with Douyin (TikTok equivalent in China), which uses AI-powered "Smart Cut" video editing. Creators selling products live can activate the feature, after which raw footage is automatically edited into

highlight reels containing product features based on when viewers engaged the most.[28] Douyin reported staggering streaming sales of RMB$1.2 trillion ($170 billion US) in 2023, with some campaigns growing by 470% year over year.[29] While the West treats live shopping as a "QVC2.0," Eastern platforms use AI to make it immersive, frictionless, and scalable, turning every seller into a potential influencer.

3.3 HYPER-PERSONALIZATION AT SCALE

AI is a real game changer when it comes to delivering personalized products and services. Today's consumers expect companies to provide them experiences that feel curated to their individual needs. Instead of a one-size-fits-all approach, AI is making it possible for companies to treat each customer uniquely, even when serving massive audiences.

While Western AI prioritizes personalization for high-value customers and patients, Eastern models focus on scaling accessibility for the upcoming user base. The future lies in blending these approaches by leveraging Western precision with Eastern inclusivity. Below are some of the key ways this is playing out in the non-Western part of the world:

- **Real-time recommendation engines:** Chinese online shopping platform Taobao uses a highly sophisticated AI recommendation system called "Guess What You Like" (猜你喜欢) to provide personalized product suggestions in real time. It applies deep learning, behavioral analytics, and reinforcement learning to analyze real-time clicks, cart additions, and even mouse hover time to make purchase suggestions with remarkable accuracy.[30] It also integrates social data from popular Chinese social media platforms, including WeChat and Weibo through indirect signals such as "shares" to prioritize recommendations trending in the user's city (e.g. "Shanghai teens are buying this lipstick"). AI-driven recommendations are central to Taobao's business model, powering over 80% of its mobile user experience (see endnote 30).

- **Personalized wellness and health tech:** Asia is pioneering AI-powered wellness solutions by seamlessly integrating modern technology with centuries-old traditional healing practices. Take Ping An's Good Doctor for example. This smart health platform uses AI to analyze symptoms through the lens of Traditional Chinese

Medicine. It can interpret pulse data from wearables to diagnose a person's health. If medication is needed, it can sync with pharmacies to autofill prescriptions, making holistic care effortless. Good Doctor has close to 400 million users; with the technology shortening diagnosis times from 15 minutes to 15 seconds, it's truly a game changer for a busy society.[31] India's HealthifyMe is another good example. Its AI coach Ria brings personalized nutrition guidance to the masses. It provides advice in ten languages, Hindi and Tamil among them, adjusting diet recommendations based on the user's locale. For street food lovers, Ria scans menus and guides users toward healthier choices. And it works! HealthifyMe claims that "95% of users who follow the diet plan & get at least some exercise into their daily routines are able to reach their target weight goal."[32]

3.4 TRANSFORMING TRADITIONAL INDUSTRIES

AI is making huge impacts in traditional sectors, including retail, agriculture, and healthcare. Here we look at two powerful examples of this transformation in the finance and education industries.

- **AI-driven fintech:** Forget Wall Street's algorithm trading platforms. The real fintech revolution is happening in the streets of Jakarta, the markets of Lagos, and the favelas of Rio. Across Asia, Africa, and Latin America, AI is reinventing the financial world as we know it; and this time, it's for the next billion users. They've begun tackling today's pressing issues, hyperinflation and cash-heavy economies among them.

MercadoLibre, often called "Latin America's Amazon," is making waves in the credit world. The company has implemented AI throughout their e-commerce operations, enabling them to provide instant credit solutions in any given scenario.[33] The algorithm utilizes its vast database to make split-second decisions, helping smoothen the loan application and agreement process. In Q1 2025, MercadoLibre reported 75% YoY credit portfolio growth, reaching almost $8 billion US.[34] This highlights the positive impact that their personalized, low-risk lending program has made.

Another example of a successful AI-powered fintech company is M-KOPA. Across Africa, over 3 million users rest easy knowing that if they face an unexpected hospitalization, instead of paying steep bills and worrying over lost income, they are insured through use of a simple yet powerful tool—their cellphones. M-KOPA is a mobile app that enables users to pay for insurance and loans continuously, in small amounts, using their cellular devices as collateral.[35] But how do they do it? "Tracking the health of our lending portfolio is an absolute bedrock competency of the organization," says CTO Owen Scott. The company utilizes machine learning to formulate an approximate timeline for each individual loan repayment, which ultimately helps protect customers while maintaining financial responsibility (see endnote 35).

These fintech solutions use AI to turn local realities—whether it's hyperinflation, cash economies, or a lacking credit history—into solutions. These platforms are proving technology's real power, transforming everyday goods and services into opportunities for financial growth.

- **Adaptive learning in edtech:** Adaptive learning is redefining the education experience by using AI to tailor lessons that meet each student's needs in real time. Asia, Africa, and Latin America are already leading with revolutionary implementations, where AI is making learning more personal and effective by adjusting content, pacing, and assessments based on how every individual student is performing.

Take Indian edtech company BYJU'S for example; it uses machine learning to analyze how students interact with lessons by tracking time spent and mistakes made. Based on this data, it adjusts lesson difficulty and switches between formats, including informational videos, text in the form of flashcards, or engaging educational games, taking into account the lowered attention span of today's generation.[36] Results show that students following AI-driven lesson plans master concepts 30% faster than with traditional methods.[37]

China's Squirrel AI takes personalization even further, breaking subjects down into 30,000+ micro-skills and pinpointing exactly where a student struggles, while further reinforcing strengths.[38] The system then generates custom exercises to fill those gaps. Studies show that in the schools where they were piloting this offering, dropout rates have already decreased by 14%.[39]

These innovations prove that AI is carrying out more than mere automation in education. By adapting to learners' unique needs no matter their location or resources, adaptive learning is making quality education more universally available than ever.

3.5 BUSINESS MODEL INNOVATION

In the past few years, we have witnessed how AI is highly effective at making existing business models more efficient. We've now gone one further, using AI to redefine how businesses operate, compete, and make money. With AI's ability to analyze vast amounts of data, automate complex tasks, and make predictions, we are unlocking entirely new ways to engage customers, deliver value, and even create new industries. We are already seeing examples of this in action; here are some of the most significant developments in AI-driven business model innovation:

- **Product-to-service transformation:** Forward-thinking companies have moved past selling products alone. Now, they are using AI to transform one-time sales into ongoing services by creating stronger ties with customers. Alibaba Cloud is a prime example; instead of intimidating small businesses with expensive software licenses, they offer AI microservices billed by usage amount. Need image recognition or language processing? You pay only for what you use, no upfront costs.[40] This flexible, pay-as-you-go approach has allowed countless resource-constrained SMEs to tap into AI tools they otherwise couldn't afford, helping lower the barrier to AI adoption. This is opening doors for smaller, newer players to compete with large enterprises and is allowing companies to build smarter, more sustainable businesses and long-term partnerships.
- **Dynamic pricing and revenue optimization:** AI is quietly transforming how businesses set prices. You have probably noticed without realizing it: maybe that jacket you've been wanting suddenly costs $50 more, or the hotel room you booked got cheaper on a rainy Tuesday. That's AI at work, constantly adjusting prices based on what's happening right now in the market. This smart pricing helps businesses stay competitive while making sure they don't leave money on the table. And for customers, it means fairer prices that reflect real-time supply and demand.
- **Personalization as a business model:** Remember when "custom-made" meant expensive and exclusive? AI is changing that. It's turning personalization into a scalable business strategy across every industry, as we saw earlier with BYJU'S and Squirrel AI. The magic lies in AI's ability to analyze individual preferences and behaviors at a massive scale. What used to require armies of human experts can now happen automatically and profitably. Customers get tailored

experiences, while businesses enjoy higher engagement and loyalty without breaking the bank.

- **AI-native marketplaces:** A new wave of marketplaces is emerging with AI programmed into their DNA. In these platforms, AI is the core engine driving everything from personalized recommendations to delivery logistics. With Pinduoduo, AI groups buyers with similar interests to unlock bulk discounts—imagine 1000 farmers teaming up to get better fertilizer prices![41] What makes marketplaces like these special? They are completely redesigning commerce using AI capabilities, creating smarter, more adaptive ways to buy and sell.
- **Social commerce:** A quiet revolution is happening in social commerce across Asia, Africa, and the Middle East. Instead of going through standalone shopping apps, the trend is shifting toward buying directly through WhatsApp statuses, TikTok videos, and WeChat moments. Take China's Xiaohongshu for example. What started as a niche platform is now Gen Z's favorite shopping hub, because it can spot micro trends before they go mainstream. That "clean girl" makeup routine or vintage sneaker collection you just discovered? Xiaohongshu's algorithms likely identified it weeks ago by analyzing millions of user posts.[42] Retail websites everywhere are beginning to incorporate a feature that lets you try on a shade of lipstick or pair of sunglasses through camera filters, with no app download needed. These markets are special because they skip the "Download Our App" phase entirely, with shopping now living in other social media apps, which people already gravitate toward daily. AI helps turn every social interaction into a potential storefront, seamlessly woven into our digital lives.

3.6 AUTONOMOUS OPERATIONS AND DECISION-MAKING

After exploring AI in today's industries, one thing becomes clear: the ultimate goal in business is AI autonomy. Companies will be able to use technology that can perceive and make decisions independently, achieving an unprecedented level of operational efficiency and agility.

- **Automated decision factories:** Think of an assembly line, but instead of widgets, it churns out thousands of decisions per second. These AI-powered systems ingest live data, analyze patterns, predict outcomes, and execute actions, all without human intervention. We are seeing it happen right now. AI fraud detection used by banks and dynamic pricing strategies in retail are prime examples of it.

> In industries like trading or cybersecurity, the speed of AI decision-making is a real game changer. Machines make split-second choices, quickly weighing pros and cons and eliminating indecisiveness. It's expected that in the future, entire business units will be running on autopilot, with human oversight concentrated on high-level strategy only. The next evolution will be when AI agents are able to learn, adapt, and make decisions off-script. We are not quite there yet, but some believe that we can achieve this soon enough for our generation to witness. Geoffrey Hinton, the "Godfather of Deep Learning," suggested that AI may surpass human reasoning in "5-20 years" in a 2023 interview after leaving Google. He also warned that once AI can self-improve, exponential progress could happen faster than expected ("years, not decades").[43] The downside is what happens when AI gets it wrong, which we will explore in the next section.

As we hand over the controls to AI, we have to ask ourselves the inevitable question: what happens when these systems get too smart? Will we end up living in the dystopian world so often portrayed in movies? Next, we will explore the hidden risks of AI, in particular, the surprising downsides of intelligence and how to handle it.

SECTION 4: THE SHADOW OF INTELLIGENCE—RISKS AND CHALLENGES IN THE AGE OF AI

AI, with all its promises, can supercharge your business. But the uncomfortable truth is that these powerful tools come with hidden dangers. The same technology that delivers enhanced efficiency, new revenue streams, and deeper customer relationships also presents complex challenges related to data quality, technology infrastructure, and the ever-evolving regulatory landscape. If we don't deal with these challenges ahead of time, the result could be devastating to every business.

One major foundational risk lies in dependency on data, as AI is only as smart as the data you feed to it. Inaccurate, incomplete, or biased data can lead to flawed AI models that generate unreliable predictions, make incorrect decisions, and double down on existing societal inequalities. For example, an HR AI bot trained purely on historical hiring data could reflect biased practices, such as favoring male candidates over their equally qualified female counterparts. A report done by IBM in 2016 estimated that poor data quality costs the US economy $3.1 trillion annually.[44] It's clear that not addressing data issues now will have a negative compounding effect on businesses later on. We will dive deeper into some common data quality and integration challenges in Chapter 2, and how companies should implement data governance, cleaning, and unification processes to maximize results.

Beyond data, companies need to face another harsh reality: AI is an energy hog, and it requires robust and scalable computing power, advanced data storage solutions, and seamless integration between AI systems and existing business applications. As we will explore in the next chapter, organizations need to audit their infrastructure capacity before investing in AI. Otherwise, it'll be like buying a sports car with no roads to drive it on.

The skills gap within the workforce is another critical risk (see Chapter 7). Most companies are woefully unprepared for the AI revolution. While 87% of leaders expect that AI will transform their business, only 19% currently have the means to make it happen.[45] Below are the top reasons why this data should be alarming to organizations:

- Middle management meltdown can be catastrophic to businesses. Middle managers are the critical bridge between a company's AI vision and successful execution—but most of them are dangerously unprepared and can't spot real AI opportunities. According to Gartner, a large number of middle managers admit to green-lighting AI projects based on vendor hype, not business impact.[46] A lack of AI literacy can lead to goal misalignment, which kills ROI and leads to sky-high adoption failure rates.
- Execution paralysis is costing businesses millions. It can be lethal when companies drown in AI planning but never ship real solutions. Gartner claims that 80% of AI pilots fail to scale, not because of weak technology, but due to a lack of the structural support necessary for company-wide integration.[47] Companies in this situation might end up with permanent "pilot purgatory," wasting millions running unscaled AI pilots without committing to full rollout. Even highly promising AI tools can fail in this way. AI investments can then easily become costly experiments with limited impact.

The global AI power struggle presents both opportunities and risks. Companies are getting caught in the crossfire of the tech cold war between the three AI superpowers, the Silicon Valley Wild West, Europe's rulebook-first approach, and China's state-directed surge. As the world plays a high-stakes game of AI chess, companies need to know which players to side with.

Finally, organizations must prepare for the long-term impacts of AI on privacy, security, and employment. In particular, the three seismic shifts we see that companies must learn to deal with are as follows:

1. The privacy paradox: AI needs data to learn and improve, but consumers are increasingly reluctant to give up their privacy, for good reason. The risk of a chatbot leak exposing millions of health and financial records certainly puts privacy at the top of the list for AI concerns.
2. The automation backlash: According to the World Economic Forum, 92 million existing jobs are expected to evolve or disappear by 2030, making way for over 170 million new roles across emerging industries.[48] The question for business leaders is not how to choose between humans and AI, but how to lead into this transition and future-proof their workforce.
3. The security arms race: On one side, attackers are leveraging AI to create more sophisticated attacks such as using convincing deepfakes. On the other side, defenders are deploying AI for automated threat responses. The concern is that AI-driven attacks can learn from failed attempts and are evolving faster than defenses. Jeffrey Hinton has famously said that AI will outsmart humans in cyberattacks in a 2023 CBS interview.[49]

While AI can transform businesses, leaders must first learn to navigate the risks that come with it. By proactively addressing issues related to data quality, skills gaps, ethical considerations, and the evolving global landscape, organizations can mitigate potential pitfalls and pave the way for a successful and responsible AI-driven future.

SECTION 5: HOW PHILOSOPHY IS THE KEY TO AI ADOPTION AND RISK MANAGEMENT IN BUSINESS

AI has the power to revolutionize our world, but it's also forcing us to address some very pressing situations:

- When algorithms decide who gets a loan or a job
- When machines start making choices we can't comprehend
- When "progress" means millions need to rebuild their careers

These answers to these questions must be collectively decided:

- Who we trust with life-changing decisions?
- What fairness really means in an automated world?
- How we stay in control of systems smarter than us?

These are deep philosophical challenges about how we shape technology, and how it, in turn, shapes us.

Ancient Chinese wisdom provides a balanced framework to navigate the disruptions, opportunities, and risks of the AI revolution. Throughout the rest of this book, we will touch on Daoism's belief in flexibility, Confucianism's responsibility, and Legalism's structured readiness. They each offer distinct yet complementary perspectives on how we should approach AI implementation in the near future.

A synthesis of wisdom: The triple lens

To manage the AI revolution responsibly:

- Daoism offers the conceptual framework to accept and balance disruption.
- Confucianism ensures preparedness and ethical integrity.
- Legalism enforces compliance and risk containment.

The AI revolution is like a fast-moving river, in Daoism's framework. Confucianism builds the bridge to cross it with care and structure. Legalism installs guardrails so no one is swept away by unchecked forces.

The future of AI in business isn't just about doing everything faster and cheaper. True progress demands balance. The Dao of AI teaches us to harmonize potential and risk, prepare ethically and structurally, and regulate firmly when needed. As the world struggles to align AI with human values, we can look to these ancient principles to help us realize that success lies in harmony, not just scale.

NOTES

1. Koch, Christof. "Constructing the Modern Mind." *Scientific American*, 2016, scientificamerican.com/article/constructing-the-modern-mind/.
2. Zwolak, Justyna. "Ada Lovelace: The World's First Computer Programmer Who Predicted Artificial Intelligence." *National Institute of Standards*

and Technology, 2023, nist.gov/blogs/taking-measure/ada-lovelace-worlds-first-computer-programmer-who-predicted-artificial.
3. O'Carroll, Eoin. "Ada Lovelace: What Did the First Computer Program Do?" *The Christian Science Monitor*, 2012, csmonitor.com/Technology/2012/1210/Ada-Lovelace-What-did-the-first-computer-program-do.
4. McCarthy, John, et al. "A Proposal for the Dartmouth Summer Research Project on Artificial Intelligence." *Chsasank*, 1955, chsasank.com/classic_papers/darthmouth-artifical-intelligence-summer-resarch-proposal.html.
5. Guarda, Dinis. "The Chronological Timeline of AI and Computing History." *Wisdomia*, 2025, wisdomia.ai/the-chronological-timeline-of-ai-and-computing-history.
6. Primary Researcher, "The First AI Winter and What The Lighthill Report Said about AI Progress." *Brightwork Research & Analysis*, 2020, brightworkresearch.com/first-ai-winter-and-what-the-lighthill-report-said-about-progress.
7. Russell, Stuart, and Peter Norvig. *Artificial Intelligence: A Modern Approach*. 4th ed., Prentice Hall, 2020.
8. Mitchell, Robin. "History of AI: Key Milestones and Impact on Technology." *Electropages*, 2025, electropages.com/blog/2025/03/history-ai-key-milestones-impact-technology.
9. Dr. Jeevanandam, Nivash. "AI Insights – Mastering Minds: A Journey into the Legacy of the Samuel Checkers Playing Program", 2024, https://indiaai.gov.in/article/mastering-minds-a-journey-into-the-legacy-of-the-samuel-checkers-playing-program-1959.
10. Katharine Miller, "From Brain to Machine: The Unexpected Journey of Neural Networks." *Stanford*, 2024, https://hai.stanford.edu/news/from-brain-to-machine-the-unexpected-journey-of-neural-networks.
11. Dwyer, Colin. "'Like A God,' Google AI Beats Human Champ Of Notoriously Complex Go Game." *National Public Radio*, 2017, npr.org/sections/thetwo-way/2017/05/23/529673475/like-a-god-google-a-i-beats-human-champ-of-notoriously-complex-go-game.
12. "AlexNet and ImageNet: The Birth of Deep Learning." *Pinecone*, pinecone.io/learn/series/image-search/imagenet/.
13. "Google Acquires Artificial Intelligence Start-Up for 500 Million Dollars." The Associated Press, https://www.cbc.ca/news/science/google-buys-deepmind-artificial-intelligence-firm-1.2512651.
14. "Cloud Tensor Processing Units (TPUs)." *Google Cloud*, cloud.google.com/tpu.
15. Pereverzieva, Olga. "Language Models, Explained: How GPT and Other Models Work." *Altexsoft*, 2025, altexsoft.com/blog/language-models-gpt/.
16. Braiek, Houssem Ben. "LLM Agents Underscore One Truth: Data Is the Real Differentiator." *Towards AI*, 2024, pub.towardsai.net/llm-agents-underscore-one-truth-data-is-the-real-differentiator-2a9a0325c546.
17. Murel, Jacob, and Eda Kavlakoglu. "What Is Transfer Learning?" *IBM*, 2024, ibm.com/think/topics/transfer-learning.
18. "Zero-Shot vs One-Shot vs Few-Shot Learning." *GeeksforGeeks*, 2025, geeksforgeeks.org/machine-learning/zero-shot-vs-one-shot-vs-few-shot-learning/.

19. Mayer, Hannah, et al. "Superagency in the Workplace: Empowering People to Unlock AI's Full Potential." *McKinsey*, 2025, mckinsey.com/capabilities/mckinsey-digital/our-insights/superagency-in-the-workplace-empowering-people-to-unlock-ais-full-potential-at-work.
20. "ET Brain: Exploring New Uses for Data and AI." *Alibaba Clouder*, 2018, https://www.alibabacloud.com/blog/et-brain-exploring-new-uses-for-data-and-ai_585388.
21. Berthiaume, Dan. "Alibaba Singles Day Performs 'in line' with $84.5 Billion Event in 2021." *Chain Store Age*, 2022, chainstoreage.com/alibaba-singles-day-performs-line-845-billion-event-2021.
22. Deliso, Meredith. "Black Friday Online Sales Dip for 1st Time, to $8.9 Billion, Adobe Finds." *ABC News*, 2021, abcnews.go.com/Business/black-friday-online-sales-dip-1st-time-89b/story?id=81422340.
23. Biondi, Annachiara. "Lessons about the Chinese Shopper from the Country's Largest Discount App." *Vogue Business*, 2019, voguebusiness.com/consumers/lessons-on-chinese-shopper-from-discount-app.
24. "PDD Holdings Revenue 2018–2025 | PDD." *Macrotrends*, 2025, macrotrends.net/stocks/charts/PDD/pdd-holdings/revenue.
25. Brown, Jordan. "Hungry for Insight: An AI Expert's Guide to Predictive Analytics for Zomato." *33rd Square*, 2024, 33rdsquare.com/tech/ai/end-to-end-predictive-analysis-on-zomato/.
26. Harkins, Nataliya. "Building an AI-Native Workforce: How to Thrive in a Digital-First Age." *Wowledge*, 2025, wowledge.com/blog/building-an-ai-native-workforce.
27. "GO-JEK: Using Machine Learning for Forecasting and Dynamic Pricing." *Terralogiq*, terralogiq.com/case-study/cloud-platform/gojek/.
28. "Douyin in 2024: Breaking News and Emerging Trends in China's Short-Video Giant." *Just One API*, 2024, justoneapi.com/post-1/post-20250802081938266.
29. "Douyin's Latest Evolution: AI, E-Commerce, and the Future of Short Video." *Just One API*, 2023, justoneapi.com/post-1/post-20250705205847969.
30. Alibaba Clouder, "How Taobao Applies AI to Personalized Recommendations." *Alibaba Cloud*, 2021, alibabacloud.com/blog/howtaobao-applies-ai-to-personalized-recommendations_597556.
31. An, Ping. "An Ecosystem to Overhaul China's Health Care." *MIT Technology Review*, 2021, technologyreview.com/2021/03/30/1021421/an-ecosystem-to-overhaul-chinas-health-care.
32. "HealthifyMe – Weightloss." *HealthifyMe*, healthifyme.com/lp/weight-loss/2/.
33. "Mercado Libre Adapted to Market Challenges, with Fintech Revenue gradually outpacing Ecommerce. Concluding Evaluation." *Amateur Investor*, 2024.
34. Elliott, Lucinda, and Kylie Madry. "Focus: MercadoLibre, Latam's Amazon.com Rival, Rides high with AI, Loans, Drones." *Reuters*, 2024, reuters.com/business/retail-consumer/mercadolibre-latams-amazoncom-rival-rides-high-with-ai-loans-drones-2024-09-30/.

35. Business Watch Team, "How Is M-Kopa Using AI To Empower Millions In Kenya?" *The Business Watch*, 2023, thebusinesswatch.com/how-is-m-kopa-using-ai-to-empower-millions-in-kenya.
36. "BYJU'S Unveils Personalized Learning Experience for Students." *Business Standard*, 2017, business-standard.com/article/news-ani/byju-s-unveils-personalized-learning-experience-for-students-117052301233_1.html.
37. "How Byju Raveendran Uses Data Analytics to Drive Success." *FasterCapital*, fastercapital.com/articles/How-Byju-Raveendran-Uses-Data-Analytics-to-Drive-Success.html.
38. "Squirrel AI Learning." *hundrED*, 2020, hundred.org/en/innovations/squirrel-ai-learning.
39. "Artificial Intelligence in the Education Sector Market Size." *Emergen Research*, 2025, emergenresearch.com/industry-report/artificial-intelligence-in-the-education-sector-market?srsltid=AfmBOoopg4XsCJ0myYUC28HRg3MTzOl4vnT4kg2TNGIZK1jlSQH7Jix&.
40. "Alibaba Cloud: A Comprehensive Guide." *Uplatz*, 2023, uplatz.com/blog/alibaba-cloud-a-comprehensive-guide/.
41. "Pinduoduo's Social Group Buying Model wins over Tier 3 & 4 Consumers." *Dao Insights*, 2020, daoinsights.com/works/pinduoduos-social-group-buying-model-wins-over-tier-3-4-consumers/.
42. 小红书技术 REDtech. "小红书高时效推荐系统背后的技术升级." *InfoQ*, 2023, xie.infoq.cn/article/8ab1eebb82450ef2f5c02b9fc.
43. Webb, Effie. "'Godfather of AI' says he's 'glad' to be 77 because the Tech Probably Won't Take over the World in His Lifetime." *Business Insider*, 2025, businessinsider.com/ai-godfather-geoffrey-hinton-superintelligence-risk-takeover-2025-4.
44. Leopold, George. "As Data Quality Declines, Costs Soar." *Datanami*, 2017, datanami.com/2017/12/13/data-quality-declines-costs-soar/. Youell, Joy. "Bad Data: The $3 Trillion-Per-Year Problem That's Actually Solvable." *Entrepreneur*, 2021, entrepreneur.com/science-technology/bad-data-the-3-trillion-per-year-problem-thats-actually/393161.
45. Global Business Development Artificial Intelligence Leadership. "McKinsey 2025 AI Report – The Urgency of Now – AI Gap – Hire Talent." *LinkedIn*, 2025, linkedin.com/pulse/mckinsey-2025-ai-report-the-urgency-bpskf/.
46. Business Wire. "Gartner Identifies Four Emerging Challenges to Delivering Value from AI Safely and at Scale." *Market Chameleon*, 2024, marketchameleon.com/PressReleases/i/1984140/IT/gartner-identifies-four-emerging-challenges-to-delivering.
47. "Business Model Innovation: A Profitable Path Forward in Uncertain Times." *Tech Mahindra*, 2025, techmahindra.com/insights/views/business-model-innovation-profitable-path-forward-uncertain-times/.
48. "就业前景." *2025 年就业未来报告, 世界经济论坛*, 2025 年, cn.weforum.org/publications/the-future-of-jobs-report-2025/in-full/2-jobs-outlook/.
49. Huddleston, Jr., Tom. "Tech Godfather Geoffrey Hinton: AI Could Rewrite Code, Escape Control." *CNBC*, 2023, cnbc.com/2023/10/11/tech-godfather-geoffrey-hinton-ai-could-rewrite-code-escape-control.html.

CHAPTER 2

The AI Readiness Framework

Many organizations are racing to implement artificial intelligence (AI) for fear of missing out or being outcompeted. However, just as many have discovered, buying the latest technology is the easy part. The real challenge is to get your entire organization up to par for AI adoption.

This chapter introduces the AI Readiness Framework (see Figure 2.1), containing seven make-or-break factors to help prepare organizations for AI readiness:

1. Data: the lifeblood of AI (quality in = quality out)
2. Technology infrastructure: AI's backbone
3. Skills: who has the capacity to run this?
4. Culture: is your team ready for change?
5. Governance: who is calling the shots?
6. Change management: how to avoid mutiny?
7. Ethics: doing well by doing good

The brutal reality facing organizations' AI ambition is that most fail at the data application stage, before they even start. According to industry research, 96% of organizations face data quality challenges in AI/ML

DOI: 10.1201/9781003644699-2

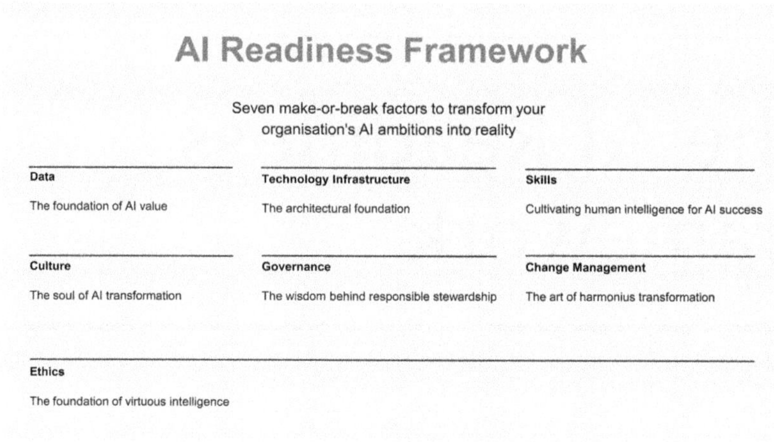

FIGURE 2.1 The AI Readiness Framework.

projects,[1] and 87% of AI projects never make it to production due to poor data quality, siloed data, or inadequate infrastructure.[2]

As we will explore later on, leading organizations can and have fixed fundamental data issues within their systems. But the honest truth is that it is nearly impossible to fix just one area at a time. To achieve your AI ambitions, all seven factors need to be developed as one, working and growing together like a well-trained orchestra. By addressing each factor using global case studies and gathering practical and effective strategies from those records, this chapter will guide you in overcoming obstacles and excelling in AI adoption.

And throughout the development of this framework, we will continue to draw inspiration from the ancient Chinese philosophical traditions that have guided leadership principles for millennia. In this chapter, we will turn to the practical application of these ancient traditions to guide our approach to building AI-ready organizations. While Chapter 1 introduced the philosophical concepts broadly, Chapter 2 demonstrates their use within specific organizational contexts and framework components.

By the end of this chapter, you'll have:

- A clear roadmap for AI readiness
- Signs to watch out for
- Practical fixes you can implement instantly
- Ancient wisdom for modern problems

AI has never been about computer abilities, but rather our ability to use it strategically in order to manifest sustainable growth. This framework provides the roadmap to help organizations develop AI capabilities that not only drive business expansion but also contribute positively to society, achieving the long-desired harmony between innovation and responsibility.

SECTION 1: DATA—THE FOUNDATION OF AI VALUE

As it turns out, the key to "winning at AI" was unknowingly discovered by builders in Mesopotamia when they decided to use limestone over mudbrick to build the ziggurat's base. They understood a fundamental truth: great structures require a strong foundation. The Anu Ziggurat at Uruk, built in 4000 BCE, still stands today, with its original limestone foundations.[3] Similarly, with AI, that foundation is data, the essential groundwork for all successful AI implementations.

1.1 THE DATA PARADOX: ABUNDANCE AMID SCARCITY

Picture this: a hospital chain with cutting-edge AI systems that is unable to deliver accurate diagnoses because its own system works against it. The paradox of modern business, especially in larger corporations, is that they are drowning in data, yet struggling for purposeful insights.

These issues are caused by what is commonly referred to as the "silo trap." Financial companies, for example, often hit a wall when they discover that their customer data is locked away in multiple legacy systems. Each system captures different aspects of customer behavior, such as transaction history, credit profiles, and digital interactions—but not a single one provides the holistic view necessary for intelligent recommendations.

When data is trapped in silos, even the smartest AI is rendered useless, creating a bureaucratic nightmare. We will look at how to break the mold and allow free movement of data later on in this section.

1.2 UNDERSTANDING DATA'S ROLE IN THE AI READINESS FRAMEWORK

Most companies don't realize how much bad data actually costs them.

- **Data scientists** spend most of their time preparing data for processing, which they could spend improving machine learning algorithms instead.

- **Governance** turns into damage control, with teams wasting a significant amount of time and effort pinpointing errors.
- **AI projects** flop because the credibility of AI-delivered results is undermined when built on data they can't trust.

Now imagine how high-quality data can multiply success.

Take Samsung Electronics' semiconductor division, for example. When they overhauled their data quality,[4] the benefit cascaded across every part of their AI framework:

- **Engineers** stopped wrestling with dirty data and started solving high-impact problems such as optimizing operations.
- **Governance** became proactive with clear data lineage, audit trail, and routine checks.
- **Change** happened faster because stakeholders saw return on investment (ROI) in real time.

Ethical AI is no longer just a checkbox. Instead, it's being built into transparent, auditable processes. The bottom line is that when you invest in data excellence first, everything else follows.

Next, let's look at how to fix data quality with practical, easy-to-follow steps from companies that have already gotten it right.

1.3 THE FOUR PILLARS OF DATA FOUNDATION

Data preparation is essentially maintaining harmony in an ecosystem. For AI to thrive, you need four elements working in balance: quality, accessibility, smooth integration, and thoughtful stewardship.

1.3.1 Quality: The Bedrock of Trust

Just as Confucian philosophy teaches us that virtue comes from daily discipline, great data quality requires constant attention. Every step of the process matters, from data collection, to validation, to routine maintenance. For AI to work, organizations must treat data quality as a strategic priority and not an IT afterthought.

The first step is to build a strategy that works. Here is a four-step, easy-to-follow implementation methodology to fix your data discrepancies and keep it in tip-top shape:

1. **Baseline Assessment:** Measure current data completeness, consistency, accuracy, and timelines across critical datasets
2. **Automated Validation:** Deploy real-time data quality checks at collection points rather than later at analysis stages
3. **Quality Metrics Dashboard:** Create visible, actionable metrics that connect data quality to business outcomes
4. **Continuous Improvement:** Establish feedback loops that identify and address quality issues systematically

Samsung's "Zero Defect" initiative provides an excellent example of how to fix your data issues the right way. As aforementioned, when their semiconductor division faced costly defects,[5] they didn't just patch over existing issues in their machines. Instead, they initiated "Zero Defect," which included automated checks on sensors, live dashboards flagging data errors before they caused problems, and a feedback loop tying production results back to data quality.[6] The result was significantly fewer defects, higher efficiency, and a renewed sense of trust in the data circulating throughout their business. If you want your AI to work, start with data you can trust.

1.3.2 Accessibility: Unlocking Silos and Supercharging Your Business

Most companies treat data like gold bars in a vault, locked away and hard to access. As a result, supply chains can't see how sales are doing, marketing makes decisions without customer service insights, and AI projects stall because critical data is stuck in another department entirely.

To allow data to be accessed by the systems and people that need it, it must be able to flow freely, like water, across departmental boundaries throughout an organization. The I Ching (易经) and Dao De Jing (道德经) both teach that water overcomes the hardest stone through persistence and finding the natural path.[7] Your data should work the same way.

These next four steps will help untrap your data and ensure information flows freely and safely:

1. **Data Flow Mapping:** Document current movement patterns of information and identify organizational barriers
2. **Integration Architecture:** Implement Application Programming Interface (API)-first platforms that enable secure, controlled data sharing
3. **Self-Service Analytics:** Provide business users with tools to access and analyze data independently
4. **Access Governance:** Establish clear protocols balancing data democratization with security requirements

Thailand's CP Group is one of Asia's largest conglomerates, operating across agribusiness, retail, and telecommunications. They have successfully managed to access their data silos and turn them into a goldmine of information. Oftentimes, the data needed is already there; it's the lack of communication between teams that renders it futile. CP Group cracked this problem with a brilliant solution. Every business unit keeps its own data, but everyone benefits from the shared flow of it.[8] In this setup, each division keeps full control of its own data, but bridges are built for safe and permission-based sharing. The payoff is less wasted inventory, sharper demand forecasts, and an AI system able to astutely spot supply chain patterns.

CP Group's use case proved that data shouldn't be hoarded, but rather should flow where it's needed throughout an organization. When done right, decisions can be reached faster, AI becomes smarter, and employees' stress goes down, while efficiency goes up.

1.3.3 Integration: Creating Unified Intelligence

Imagine trying to complete a puzzle where every piece is locked in a different room—that's what working with disconnected data feels like. True power comes when we bring all those pieces together in a way that actually makes sense. Daoist philosophy teaches us that true understanding comes from seeing how everything connects (道生一, 一生万物). The same applies to data: isolated numbers are meaningless, but unified information becomes intelligence.

Here are the steps to transforming isolated data sources into comprehensive, actionable intelligence:

1. **Data Architecture Design:** Create a unified schema that accommodates diverse data sources while maintaining source system integrity
2. **ETL/ELT Pipelines:** Implement robust extract, transform, load processes that ensure data consistency and timeliness
3. **Master Data Management:** Establish authoritative sources for critical business entities (customers, products, locations)
4. **Real-Time Integration:** Deploy streaming architectures for applications requiring immediate data updates

Now let's look at Emirates Airlines, the maestro of aviation data. With a fleet of 260+ jets flying to over 140 destinations worldwide,[9,10] Emirates handles an abundance of data: passenger preferences from millions of bookings, real-time fuel stats from every aircraft, weather systems across continents … the list goes on and on. They adopted a brilliant data integration system that brings all information together in one unified platform,[11] which translates between different systems seamlessly. Data is updated in real time so that every decision is based on fresh statistics.[60] The results have been nothing short of spectacular: increased accuracy in predicting mechanical issues before they happen, money saved through optimized fuel use, and smoother journeys thanks to personalized passenger experiences. Emirates proves that the path to success starts with integrated data.

1.3.4 The Core of AI Readiness: Building a Resilient Data Foundation

Data excellence is a never-ending race you cannot afford to lose. Data quality, quantity, and management must stay at peak performance, constantly adapting and updating to keep up with evolving standards. The reality of data excellence is that it's not a one-time project. It is an ongoing discipline that concerns every part of your business.

AI is only as good as the data that powers it. You can choose to be the organization that wastes time and resources chasing advanced AI without first getting your data in order, or create a lasting competitive edge by building on a solid data foundation. The choice is yours.

SECTION 2: TECHNOLOGY INFRASTRUCTURE—THE ARCHITECTURAL FOUNDATION

Ancient Chinese architects had a golden rule, "Tian Di" (天地). It represents the art of balancing soaring ambitions with well-grounded foundations. They understood that the most breathtaking pagodas needed the structural genius to stay standing throughout the dynasties.

The same wisdom is also applicable to AI development today. You may have sky-high AI ambitions, but they will only succeed if they are built on equally strong technological infrastructure, which serves as the critical bridge between your data foundation and AI capabilities.

Premium gasoline is only viable with certain engines. The same goes for data. Your data carries great potential, but only the right technology infrastructure can transform it into action. In this section, we will explore how to bridge the gap between the two to help unlock your full AI potential.

2.1 THE INFRASTRUCTURE PARADOX: POWER AND COMPLEXITY

When it comes to modern AI infrastructure, on the one hand, cloud platforms have made supercomputing power easily accessible, sometimes with a simple swipe of your credit card. But on the other hand, the complexity of implementing and managing these systems has increased exponentially. It's actually harder than ever to make them work well for existing business operations.

The I Ching's central teaching is that change is the only constant in the universe[12]; this proves especially relevant for AI infrastructure planning. The old IT rulebook valued stability above all things. However, AI demands constant change and experimentation, which is the exact opposite. This philosophical shift requires Yin Yang balance, which means harmonizing stability with innovation, security with accessibility, and efficiency with experimentation. India's Tata Consultancy Services (TCS) has managed this balance very well.

As one of the world's largest IT service companies, TCS has faced the challenge of modernizing infrastructure for internal operations, involving its 600,000+ employees,[13] along with serving its diverse client requirements across industries. TCS embraced the challenge and adopted the change through what they call "contextual infrastructure"—technology platforms that automatically adjust based on workload requirements, security contacts, and business priorities.[14] Their efforts paid off. They experienced a significant reduction in infrastructure costs, faster deployment of new AI applications, and a sizeable improvement in resource utilization efficiency.

Most importantly, they are now able to adopt new technology, such as quantum computing, without starting from scratch.

2.2 THE FOUR PILLARS OF AI-READY INFRASTRUCTURE

How can we prepare our infrastructure for future AI needs as TCS did? Well, an effective AI framework depends on the balance of four interdependent elements: a computational foundation, storage architecture, an integration platform, and operational excellence.

2.2.1 Computational Foundation: Processing Power for Intelligence

At the heart of every great AI system lies a rock-solid computational foundation. It's the powerhouse that turns raw data into real intelligence. Constructing a foundation that meets current requirements is not difficult. However, the real challenge is to build an infrastructure that is fast, flexible, and capable of scaling for tomorrow's breakthroughs.

Here is a condensed version of how to build the computational foundation that has the processing power for tomorrow's intelligence needs:

1. **Workload Assessment:** Analyze current and projected computational AI requirements across different use cases and time horizons
2. **Hybrid Architecture Design:** Combine cloud services with on-premises infrastructure and edge computing based on performance, cost, and security requirements
3. **Auto-Scaling Implementation:** Deploy dynamic resource allocation systems that adjust computational capacity based on demand patterns
4. **Performance Optimization:** Implement tools that track performance levels and maximize hardware utilization while minimizing computational waste

South Korea's Naver, operator of the country's top search engine and digital ecosystem, runs on a computational foundation designed for a massive scale and intelligence level. Naver supports over 700 million active monthly users across online search,[15] shopping, and messaging services. Its infrastructure handles billions of monthly searches and nonstop AI training for smarter real-time recommendations. The secret to their success? A hybrid system that blends heavy AI training with edge computing for data-based, instant decisions.[16] During the holiday shopping season, when traffic spikes, Naver can auto-scale in minutes with no lag. Naver's success has demonstrated that a smarter computational foundation produces faster AI, which brings happier users.

2.2.2 Storage Architecture: Organizing Information at Scale

The data to be used by AI must be stored properly in order to run smoothly. Storage architecture needs to provide the capacity, but most importantly, it also needs to provide effortless access to the right information at the right time.

To build a storage layer that can scale effortlessly for growing AI models, apply the following four design principles:

1. **Data Lifecycle Analysis:** Map data usage patterns to determine appropriate storage tiers and access requirements
2. **Tiered Storage Implementation:** Deploy automated systems that move data between storage types based on business rules and cost optimization
3. **Access Pattern Optimization:** Implement caching and preloading features that anticipate data requirements for an AI application
4. **Backup and Recovery:** Establish comprehensive data protection systems that ensure business continuity without compromising performance

Tiered data storage is a well-established practice in data management. To face the challenge of managing large volumes of data spanning multiple industries and business functions, a storage solution was designed based on data access patterns. Hot data, that is, frequently used data, sits on lightning-fast SSDs. Warm data (accessed weekly) lives on budget-friendly disks, while cold data, stored in the long term, stays in cheap archives.[17]

Data is automatically shuffled to where it belongs, ensuring active AI models get instant access to what they need. This system has allowed companies in the farming, retail, and logistics industries, among others, to develop all-around smarter AI solutions. When your storage works smarter, your whole business can run more smoothly.

2.2.3 Integration Platform: Connecting Diverse Systems

Think of integration platforms as the ultimate AI matchmakers. They are the reason your data and applications can finally "talk" to each other without chaos. Effective integration works wonders for AI: your customer relationship management "chats" with supply chain data, and legacy systems dance with cloud apps in perfect sync. No more data silos; just one big, happy family of data!

A Chinese Siheyuan (四合院) is a courtyard fully enclosed by buildings. Each structure has its own purpose, whether it be a kitchen, study, or bedroom, and they all connect seamlessly around a shared center.[18] This architectural principle can be applied to systems within your company. Here is a four-step checklist to help you design one of your own:

1. **System Inventory:** Catalog all existing technology systems, data formats, and integration requirements across the organization
2. **API Strategy Development:** Design standardized interfaces that enable secure, efficient communication between different systems
3. **Integration Testing:** Implement comprehensive testing frameworks that ensure reliability and performance under varying load conditions
4. **Security Framework:** Establish authentication, authorization, and encryption standards that protect data during system integration

The complexity of operating across diverse systems can in reality be turned into a competitive advantage. When managed well, it enables seamless cross-platform experiences that competitors with simpler structures cannot easily copy.

2.2.4 Operational Excellence: Sustaining Performance

AI infrastructure thrives on discipline, precision, and constant refinement. This is where operational excellence comes in. When done right, it not only keeps systems running smoothly, but most importantly, it evolves with your growing AI needs. Just as self-cultivation requires daily discipline, a company's infrastructure demands relentless care. Below are the key disciplines that will keep your infrastructure operating above industry standards:

1. **Monitoring Implementation:** Deploy comprehensive monitoring systems that track performance, security, and reliability metrics across all infrastructure components

2. **Automation Development:** Implement automated responses to common operational issues
3. **Continuous Improvement:** Establish regular review processes that identify and implement infrastructure enhancements
4. **Disaster Recovery:** Create robust backup and recovery systems that ensure business continuity under various failure scenarios

Implementing a kaizen ("continuous improvement")-powered operational framework by consistently prioritizing tiny tweaks to disruptive overhauls leads to exponential improvement over time.

Through these efforts, it is further demonstrated that the key to operational excellence is not being perfect all the time. It's about building a system that has the ability to evolve through continuous improvement.

2.3 ENABLING COMPREHENSIVE AI READINESS

Technology infrastructure serves as the critical enabler for all other components of the AI Readiness Framework. Without strong computational foundations, skilled practitioners cannot develop and deploy sophisticated AI solutions effectively. Without accessible integration platforms, cultural transformation stalls because employees cannot access the tools and insights necessary for data-driven decision-making. Without the method of continuous improvement over time, governance frameworks become reactive rather than proactive because infrastructure issues consume resources that should be used for strategic oversight.

Consider the holistic impact demonstrated by China's Alibaba Group, which built a comprehensive AI infrastructure to support its e-commerce services, cloud computing, and logistics operations. They plan on investing the equivalent of $53 billion USD over the next three years, creating the technological foundation necessary for remarkable AI innovations across multiple domains.[19]

Alibaba's infrastructure enables their AI systems to process over 500,000 transactions per second during peak shopping events,[20] provide real-time language translation for international customers,[21] optimize logistic routes for millions of daily package deliveries, and detect fraudulent transactions with high accuracy.[22] More importantly, the flexibility of their infrastructure supports continuous innovation; new AI applications can be deployed within days rather than months, experimental technologies can be tested without disrupting production systems, and emerging AI capabilities can be integrated rapidly as soon as they become available.

2.4 THE PATH FORWARD: INFRASTRUCTURE AS A STRATEGIC FOUNDATION

Despite how important technology infrastructure is as the foundation for properly managing data and building skills, organizations must avoid prioritizing technical specifications over practical needs. Infrastructure must support skilled practitioners, enable cultural adoption, facilitate governance, and most importantly align with ethical principles. Investing in resilient infrastructure ensures harmonious integration of human expertise and AI, which is the key to long-term success.

SECTION 3: SKILLS—CULTIVATING HUMAN INTELLIGENCE FOR AI SUCCESS

The Confucian idea that "lifelong learning brings enduring fulfilment (学而时习之, 不亦说乎)"[23] serves as a reminder that mastery is a continuous journey. This wisdom feels especially relevant today, in the age of AI. The most successful companies know that AI readiness is not about having the latest algorithms, but rather that it's important to build the right human skills to be able to use the technology effectively. Whether it is technical know-how, analytical thinking, or strategic decision-making, human skills are what truly give AI its power to make a difference.

Investing in skills does not only boost performance. It helps organizations shape the culture, strengthen governance, and manage change smoothly. When it all comes together, organizations are able to thrive amidst today's chaos.

3.1 THE SKILLS EVOLUTION: PREPARING FOR WHAT COMES NEXT

Traditional skill development focuses on mastering functional expertise within stable domains. AI systems, however, evolve continuously, which demands ongoing learning in order to harness new capabilities. AI systems often span across different organizational roles, so cross-functional literacy is critical. As human–AI collaboration becomes the new baseline, a fundamentally different skills approach is required.

Singapore's GovTech understood this shift clearly and developed its strategy accordingly. Recognizing AI's involvement across all public sector functions, from healthcare to urban development, the government adopted an "AI for everyone" initiative.[24] Rather than creating separate AI specialist roles, GovTech developed AI-augmented capabilities within existing job functions.[25] Urban planners developed skills in geospatial AI for traffic optimization. Customer service representatives gained competencies in AI-assisted client support. This approach created organization-wide AI literacy while maintaining area-specific expertise.

The payoff? Faster response times and notably sharper policy insights. Equipping your workforce with AI skills opens doors for a new form of professional agility where humans and AI can co-evolve.

3.2 THE THREE DIMENSIONS OF AI SKILLS EXCELLENCE

Chinese educational philosophy values well-rounded growth in intellectual, practical, and moral development. From this, we can deduce that cultivating strong AI skills requires a focus on three key areas: technical proficiency, analytical intelligence, and strategic wisdom.

Technical proficiency means having the hands-on skills to build and maintain AI systems. Unlike traditional IT roles that prioritize domain specialty, working with AI requires adaptability, including experimentation, refinement, and constant learning.

Analytical intelligence is all about making sense of AI's outputs by spotting key patterns and turning technical insights into real business results.

Strategic wisdom bridges technical know-how with big-picture thinking. This skill helps leaders make smart calls on AI investments, rollouts, and governance.

Mastering these AI skills is not a one-time effort. Just as leading organizations invest in continuous upskilling, businesses and governments need a structured yet adaptable framework to keep pace with AI's rapid evolution. The Continuous Cultivation Approach introduced below is a dynamic approach designed to systematically develop and refine AI capabilities at every level, ensuring long-term competitiveness.

3.3 IMPLEMENTATION METHODOLOGY: THE CONTINUOUS CULTIVATION APPROACH

Successful skill development plans recognize that individual capabilities must connect to broader organizational and societal objectives. Laid out below are the four key phases for an organization to implement a successful skills strategy:

Phase 1: Foundation Assessment involves a comprehensive evaluation of current capabilities across technical, analytical, and strategic dimensions. Organizations must identify skill gaps not only in traditional AI roles but across all functions that will interact with AI systems.

Phase 2: Targeted Development implements role-specific training programs that build upon existing expertise while adding AI-enhanced capabilities. Rather than replacing current skills, this approach integrates AI competencies to go along with functional knowledge.

Phase 3: Practical Application ensures that skill development connects directly to real business challenges and opportunities. Learning through actual AI implementation projects creates a deeper understanding of how to apply one's knowledge in various scenarios and allows for reinforcement and retention of these skills.

Phase 4: Continuous Evolution establishes ongoing learning systems that adapt to emerging AI technologies and changing business requirements. This reflects the Confucian understanding that mastery requires a lifelong commitment to improvement.

AI in business cannot progress through individual improvement alone. It requires collective contribution toward a larger purpose.

3.4 ENABLING FRAMEWORK INTEGRATION

Development of technical skills is critical in turning infrastructure investment into real-world solutions. Analytical intelligence fuels a culture that trusts data over a gut feeling. Strategic wisdom ensures governance and ethics move in tandem with innovation.

Take PingAn Insurance for example. Their multi-billion-dollar AI transformation didn't happen on account of their technology, but rather the people behind it. Skills training is the spark that brought this already AI-equipped organization to life. As of 2024, they employed over 20,000 software engineers and 3000 scientists,[26] creating a workforce that is not only capable of using AI tools but is also able to evolve with the technology. Through this transformation, PingAn sparked a cultural shift toward data-driven decision-making, airtight governance for complex deployments, and ethical AI servicing beyond 240 million customers.[27]

This mirrors the Chinese ideal of the "Jun Zi" (君子), which represents an exemplary person with balanced knowledge, skill, and wisdom. In AI readiness, that means winning is all about having the most capable team behind you. Invest in people, and success will follow.[28]

SECTION 4: CULTURE—THE SOUL OF AI TRANSFORMATION

The Chinese term "文化," meaning "culture," is fascinating. It combines "文" (literacy/civilization) and "化" (to transform). Its original meaning was "the process of transforming people through education." The term embodies the Chinese philosophy that true change is never forced, but cultivated gradually (以文化人).[29] This wisdom proves especially relevant in business, in which strong corporate culture isn't created through rigid rules, but emerges organically from how employees naturally operate.

4.1 THE CULTURAL PARADOX: INNOVATION WITHIN TRADITION

Modern organizations face a fundamental cultural paradox: AI thrives on experimentation, but most established cultures prioritize predictability and proven approaches. This cultural tug-of-war reflects the Daoist principle of Yin Yang, which stresses that the solution always lies in finding a dynamic balance, as opposed to choosing sides.

South Korea's LG Electronics successfully navigated this paradox. As a traditional Korean manufacturer, LG faced the typical resistance to change; customers ignored AI recommendations, as they preferred to rely solely on their own intuition. Practiced engineers dismissed predictive maintenance, favoring traditional methods instead.

LG's breakthrough started with their "Affectionate Intelligence" program, which linked AI innovations to existing organizational values rather than replacing them.[30] For example, it framed AI as the digital ally of craftsmanship and positioned AI quality control as a sworn commitment to customer satisfaction.

This approach transformed AI from a disruptive force into a natural evolution of established strengths. The real win with these breakthroughs is the collective acceptance of AI as a core capability. Employees begin inventing new AI use cases themselves, and change ceases to feel like a threat.

4.2 THE THREE PILLARS OF AI-READY CULTURE

Drawing from Chinese philosophical traditions that emphasize balanced development across intellectual, emotional, and behavioral dimensions, effective transformation of people's attitude toward AI requires bringing together three core pillars: mindset evolution, collaborative intelligence, and continuous learning.

Mindset Evolution requires rethinking the human–AI dynamic: from "us vs. AI" to "us alongside AI." Most traditional cultures still see humanity and AI as rivals, but forward-thinking companies are proving that the magic happens when we combine strengths, with AI bringing speed, data processing, and pattern recognition, while humans contribute to creativity, empathy, and real-world judgment. When AI is no longer treated as a threat and is seen as a tool, the benefits are shared by everyone.

Collaborative Intelligence involves reanalyzing the company's org chart to break down the traditional data silos. Most companies keep their tech teams, business units, and frontline workers in separate bubbles. But for AI to reach its full potential, companies not only need to combine human and AI capabilities effectively, but also need to cross the restrictive boundaries through different company functions and hierarchy levels. Game-changing innovations, such as AI systems that connect retail demand with logistics, became possible only when business units worked together. For example, the AI that matches retail demand with supply trucks, warehouses, and even hotel kitchens didn't come from one team. It came from bringing multiple business units together to share data and intelligence.

Continuous Learning requires the establishment of an "AI learning loop." The traditional one-time "training day" will no longer work, as AI demands constant experimentation and improvement. Learning should not be an "event," but instead should be part of your company's fabric. Establish a monthly pause of regular activities to explore AI. Instead of boring lectures, organize hands-on and role-specific workshops. When encouraged, learning becomes contagious, which promotes initiative and collaborative growth amidst a period of rapid change.

4.3 IMPLEMENTATION METHODOLOGY: THE ORGANIC TRANSFORMATION APPROACH

Like any initiative with the ultimate goal of initiating cultural change, the big bang approach rarely works. Forcing AI adoption typically backfires. Smart companies are doing it gradually, promoting organic changes that align with existing organizational values while gently redirecting individuals toward AI-ready practices.

The first important step to organic AI transformation is cultural assessment; diagnose before you prescribe. Map an org chart to understand who really influences decisions; discover resistance patterns to identify habits that kill innovation; find cultural strengths that support AI adoption. Keep in mind that your best allies are likely already there; you simply have yet to identify them.

The next step is to align values; make AI feel less foreign. Don't pile on new values. Instead, connect AI initiatives to your existing organizational identity. For example, if customer obsession is a core value, show how AI predicts customers' needs before they are voiced.

Behavioral integration is also key; changing group behavior can be difficult without backlash. Blend AI into routine rhythms while encouraging debate that draws on human experience. A more unique approach would be to adjust promotion criteria to recognize AI–human collaboration and management.

The final phase is cultural evolution. That is, creating the "viral" effect that encourages people to come on board. Create self-reinforcing cycles to make AI-ready behaviors stick without imposed requirements. Turn early adopters into AI evangelists by giving them the platform to spread enthusiasm and lead AI initiatives. Success stories are an effective practice to let culture change happen on its own, by way of peer momentum. With the right push, AI adoption becomes a mindset rather than a mandate, with growth and skill adjustment coming naturally.

4.4 ENABLING FRAMEWORK SYNERGY

The most powerful cultural transformations occur through gentle, persistent influence rather than forceful imposition. Employees adopt what they help shape. Innovation sticks when it feels familiar. Ethics thrive in cultures of shared purpose. Each component of your AI strategy is amplified.

A collectively AI-ready mindset emerges when organizations recognize and honor their existing strengths while gradually cultivating new capabilities, creating environments where human intelligence and AI flow naturally toward shared organizational objectives. The right culture turns AI investments from cost centers into value creators, empowering teams, satisfying customers, and securing your company's future.

SECTION 5: GOVERNANCE—THE WISDOM BEHIND RESPONSIBLE STEWARDSHIP

"治国 (Zhi Guo)," the art of statecraft, teaches that great leadership balances strength with compassion, order with adaptability, and short-term gains with lasting prosperity. Confucius's concept of benevolent governance, or "仁政," goes even further. It teaches that true power lies in naturally creating conditions where people can thrive and feel respected.

These principles resonate deeply in AI governance today, applying to both the people and innovations within a company. Organizations must build oversight that unlocks AI's potential while guarding against risks that erode trust, compliance, and long-term value.

5.1 GOVERNING THE UNPREDICTABLE: BALANCING INNOVATION AND CONTROL

AI presents a unique governance paradox: the more powerful a tool it becomes, the harder it is to control with traditional methods. We are dealing with systems that evolve in real-time, making conventional rulebooks obsolete almost as soon as they are written.

The Daoist principle of "无为而治," governing by stepping back, highlights the right approach to solving the issue. The best AI governance is less about rigid control and more about creating guardrails that allow innovation to flourish safely.

The Monetary Authority of Singapore offered a blueprint with their groundbreaking Model AI Governance Framework implemented across the nation's financial sector. They developed principle-based governance,[31] replacing micromanagement with clearly set outcomes stating that:

- AI decisions must be explainable
- Data integrity must be maintained
- Risks must be proactively managed
- Stakeholders must stay informed

Financial institutions could then design their own paths to achieve these standards. As a result of the new approach, AI-related compliance issues dropped drastically, and customer trust in AI-powered services grew as transparency improved. And AI 'isn't slowing itself down—with strong risk management in place, companies invite change more confidently, not less.

5.2 ITERATIVE IMPLEMENTATION FOR AI GOVERNANCE SUCCESS

AI governance isn't built overnight. The most effective approach mirrors how AI itself improves: through gradual, iterative refinement that leverages what works while adapting to new challenges.

The first step is to lay the foundation. Start with what you already have. Strengthen existing risk and compliance frameworks to address basic AI oversight needs. Take stock of current capabilities, identify AI-specific gaps, and establish clear accountability.

Next, develop your framework. With the basics in place, you have the opportunity to create tailored governance for AI. In this phase, you will define ethical principles, build processes for algorithmic accountability, and implement risk assessment tools.

Then it's time to make it operational. Transition from policy to practice by building governance into daily workflows, making requirements feel natural and less bureaucratic, and ensuring that tools are actively applied, not just outlined.

Lastly is a tactic that has been, and will continue to be, a key focus throughout this book: continuous evolution. Treat governance as a living system. Run it through regular framework checkups, engage in active stakeholder feedback loops, and continuously adapt your approach to new technology and business regulations.

The bottom line is that your style of governance should mature alongside your AI capabilities, with each reinforcing the other in an upward spiral of trust and innovation.

5.3 ENABLING FRAMEWORK HARMONY

Proper AI governance weaves together all aspects of your AI Readiness Framework. In the end, you will be left with four optimized components that work in harmony:

- **Data** that is both powerful and private
- **Infrastructure** built for innovation and compliance
- **Skills** that include technical mastery and ethical judgment
- **Culture** that drives progress while protecting value

South Korea's financial powerhouse, KB Financial Group, delivers a masterclass in integration. Their governance framework creates unified data standards across their banking, insurance, and security sectors. It aligns tech investments with regulatory needs, bakes ethics directly into AI training programs, and reinforces cultural values around customer protection and fairness.[32] They have deployed their AI system at scale while actively increasing stakeholder trust, proving that governance should be an accelerator and not a roadblock.

The golden rule of governance is to build genuine commitment to doing AI right. And *that's* when it becomes a competitive advantage.

SECTION 6: CHANGE MANAGEMENT—THE ART OF HARMONIOUS TRANSFORMATION

Change management can make or break AI success. You may have all the technical pieces in place: perfect data, cutting-edge infrastructure, skilled teams, and a supportive culture, but without thoughtful change management, even the most brilliant AI solutions can crash against human resistance. The most successful organizations approach change by finding the path of least resistance while staying true to core objectives.

Great change management aligns human capabilities with technological advancement. This way, operational continuity is maintained during transitional periods, and genuine confidence is built at each step of the way. This foundation becomes especially crucial when we reach ethical considerations in the next section, because *how* you change matters just as much as *what* you change. The organizations that master this balance will achieve transformations that last because they grow naturally from within.

6.1 THE TRANSFORMATION IMPERATIVE: NAVIGATING HUMAN DYNAMICS IN AI ADOPTION

AI adoption represents perhaps the most profound workforce transformation since the Industrial Revolution. But unlike in the past, where machines replaced manual labor, today's revolution targets cognitive work. This creates unique psychological and organizational dynamics that demand:

- **Cognitive empathy:** Understanding that AI threatens professional identities in ways physical automation never did
- **Psychological safety nets:** Creating spaces where employees can voice fears without judgment
- **Redefined value propositions:** Clearly articulating what humans bring to the table in human–AI partnerships

Effective change management requires approaches that are sophisticated enough to address the above demands while still being practical to implement, as demonstrated in Commonwealth Bank's case study below.

As Australia's largest bank, they had to face this challenge head-on by developing a radical new playbook that addressed the needs of their

52,000 employees[33] amidst a period of fast-paced AI adoption. Their adaptive change framework prioritized tackling AI anxiety before teaching technical skills,[34] and redefined jobs as dynamic partnerships with AI. Culturally, experimentation became an accepted part of the learning process, and all stakeholders were kept engaged through constant evolution.

The transformation transformed itself. What started as an AI adoption program became something far more powerful, and the team was able to move from adoption to innovation as their confidence grew.

6.2 THE FOUR PILLARS OF AI CHANGE MANAGEMENT

Effective AI change management requires attention to four fundamental pillars: human readiness, capability cultivation, cultural harmonization, and stakeholder orchestration.

Human readiness: Successful AI implementation starts with the people involved. This pillar focuses on building the right mindset to serve as the foundation teams need in order to adopt AI tools with confidence. As we explored before, DBS Bank had an effective approach to transforming AI anxiety into conviction, which included:

- Regular opportunities to pause and reflect
- Dedicated support channels for AI concerns
- Hands-on workshops to build familiarity

By addressing the human side of digital transformation first, DBS created an environment where employees felt that they were equipped and supported for the change, resulting in a smoother transition.

Capability cultivation: AI adoption requires new ways of thinking and collaborating. This pillar focuses on developing the unique competencies employees need to work effectively alongside AI systems. It's critical for employees to know (a) when to trust (and question) AI outputs, and (b) how to augment, not replace, human judgment.

Cultural harmonization: This pillar focuses on how AI strengthens the unique traits of an organization while creating space for new approaches to work. By viewing AI as a cultural amplifier rather than a disruptor, companies get to maintain their personal style and standards while gaining new skills and considering new perspectives. Hence, innovation feels more authentic, and not imposed.

Stakeholder orchestration: This pillar ensures that transformation works for everyone, from frontline employees to community partners. Canada's Royal Bank knows how to align transformation across all touchpoints[35]:

- Employees have a clear pathway to AI-augmented roles
- Customers receive clarification of AI benefits/drawbacks
- Regulators engage in proactive compliance partnerships
- Communities organize responsible innovation commitments

Royal Bank proves that the most sustainable change happens when all parties impacted are aligned.

6.3 IMPLEMENTATION METHODOLOGY: THE ADAPTIVE APPROACH

Successful AI change management navigates transformation according to natural circumstances, such as existing workflows and cultural norms. It responds to changing conditions and adjusts course when needed. This adaptive approach beats rigid planning every time. There are four phases in this framework to help you achieve fluidity:

Phase 1: Readiness Assessment—Before any tech rollout, smart leaders will conduct a pulse survey to:

- Map existing change capacity and AI readiness
- Identify both vocal and silent stakeholder concerns
- Pinpoint where AI will create the most value (and disruption)

This discovery phase is all about listening to your data and your people, adopting a wide stance to uncover hidden worries you may have overlooked.

Phase 2: Foundation Building—With insights in hand, shift focus to:

- Creating learning environments where failure is encouraged
- Developing crystal-clear communication about your AI journey
- Building robust support systems for employees amidst change

The goal is to establish safety and trust before introducing new tools.

Phase 3: Guided Adaptation—Now the real work begins, through:

- Hands-on, bite-sized AI experiences
- Peer coaching and early success celebrations
- Continuous feedback loops for course correction

This is the phase where competence and confidence grow together, at a pace that acknowledges and respects the learning curve.

Phase 4: Sustainable Integration—This final phase focuses on:

- Incorporating AI naturally into daily workflows
- Establishing communities for ongoing learning
- Recognizing and incentivizing effective human–AI collaboration

With the conclusion of this phase, the goal then shifts from managing change to enabling ongoing adaptation as AI capabilities continue to evolve.

6.4 ENABLING FRAMEWORK SYNERGY

AI change management is the vital link between your technology investment and the people who will use it. Truly effective change management makes data initiatives feel transparent, ensures infrastructure works for people (not just engineers), and tailors skills development to how people actually learn. The secret lies in balancing what technology can do and what people need. This harmony creates the foundation for transformative success that benefits all stakeholders.

SECTION 7: AI ETHICS—THE FOUNDATION OF VIRTUOUS INTELLIGENCE

Think of AI ethics as your organization's conscience in digital form. They are what ensure your smart systems stay aligned with human values, not just business goals. Ethics cannot be treated as an afterthought, because AI without ethics is like a car without brakes. It is simply too powerful to be left uncontrolled.

7.1 THE ETHICAL IMPERATIVE: BALANCING INNOVATION WITH MORAL RESPONSIBILITY

Technology is only as good as the values that guide it. As AI gets smarter, we must work harder to keep systems fair and unbiased, protect people's privacy, and make sure AI decisions people can understand.

Rakuten has proven that it is 100% possible to innovate quickly while acting responsibly. Their AI ethics charter[36] addresses algorithm fairness, privacy protection, and transparency requirements. Along with seeing fewer bias complaints and having faster rollout of trusted AI services, their use case proves that putting the guardrails down doesn't limit innovation. When channeled responsibly, it helps companies build the kind of AI people are actually willing to use.

7.2 THE FUNDAMENTAL PILLARS OF AI ETHICS

Effective AI ethics require the following essential guardrails:

Fairness first: This ensures that AI systems treat all individuals fairly. "Bias bounty" programs are the perfect example.[37] They pay people to uncover algorithmic discrimination, such as in job recruitment and performance evaluation processes.

Privacy by design: In other words, protecting individual data rights without limiting a system's valuable applications. Systems need to be equipped with "blind learning," where they can analyze customer trends without seeing personal data.

Human oversight: Maintaining human agency in AI-enhanced environments. Examples include Qatar's National Bank, where their AI co-pilot system flags unusual transactions for human review later on.[38]

7.3 BUILDING ETHICAL AI: A PRACTICAL BLUEPRINT

Creating responsible AI is not a theoretical exercise; below is a structured step-by-step process on how to do it:

1. Set down your moral foundation. In this step, define clear ethical principles tailored to your organization.
2. Now, systematically integrate those principles. Embed ethical checks at every stage in the development process.
3. Stay vigilant. Regularly testing for unintended outcomes is critical.

4. Measure impact. It's important to track how and how much your AI actually affects people and communities. This will help you create a positive feedback loop.

When ethics drive your AI strategy, a ripple effect is triggered that transforms every part of your business, ensuring technology better serves your people.

CONCLUSION: THE HARMONY OF COMPREHENSIVE READINESS

The ancient Chinese wisdom, "知行合一 (Zhi Xing He Yi)," means unity of knowledge and action. It reminds us that understanding AI's potential means nothing without systematic implementation. The seven-component AI Readiness Framework demonstrates that sustainable AI success requires harmonious development across the areas of data, technology infrastructure, skills, culture, governance, change management, and ethics holistically, rather than having isolated excellence in any single domain.

Similar to the interwoven branches of a mighty tree, these framework elements strengthen each other through mutual reinforcement. Data quality improves when supported by robust governance; cultural transformation accelerates when guided by ethical principles; change management succeeds when backed by comprehensive skill development. The Confucian principle of "中庸之道," the Doctrine of the Mean, teaches that excellence emerges through balanced cultivation rather than leaning toward extremes.

Organizations embarking on an AI transformation journey must resist the temptation of piecemeal approaches that prioritize individual technical capabilities while neglecting the importance of collective growth. True AI readiness requires patient, systematic attention to all framework components, developing organizational capabilities that can evolve alongside today's rapidly advancing industries and technologies.

The path forward demands both ancient wisdom and modern innovation, honoring timeless principles of human flourishing while embracing new and promising technological possibilities. When organizations achieve this harmony, AI becomes not merely a tool for competitive advantage but also a force for organizational and societal advancement.

NOTES

1. Roedner, Don. "Why 96% of Enterprises Face AI Training Data Issues." *Dataconomy*, 2019, dataconomy.com/2019/07/30/why-96-of-enterprises-face-ai-training-data-issues/.
2. V.P. Staff, "Why Do 87% of Data Science Projects Never Make It into Production?" *VentureBeat*, 2019, venturebeat.com/ai/why-do-87-of-data-science-projects-never-make-it-into-production/.
3. "Ana Waqar, Lost in Time: Uruk." *Rethinking The Future*, re-thinkingthefuture.com/case-studies/a8565-lost-in-time-uruk/.
4. A.D. "Big Data Revolutionizing Samsung Operations and Product Development." *Harvard Business School*, 2023, d3.harvard.edu/platform-digit/submission/big-data-revolutionizing-samsung-operations-and-product-development/.
5. Mude, Gnani Prathap Naik. "The Role of AI in Legacy Software Application Modernization." *International Journals of Multidisciplinary Research Academy*, 2024, ijmra.us/project%20doc/2024/IJMT_MARCH2024/IJMTMarch24.pdf.
6. Masood, Adnan. "AI Use-Case Compass – Manufacturing: Smart Factories, Zero Downtime." *Medium*, 2025, medium.com/%40adnanmasood/ai-use-case-compass-manufacturing-smart-factories-zero-downtime-c8a72067fc3f.
7. Stenudd, Stefan. "Tao Te Ching Chapter 78." *The Taoist Classic by Lao Tzu Translated and Explained*, 2015, taoistic.com/taoteching-laotzu/taoteching-78.htm.
8. Charoen Pokphand Group. *Sustainability Report 2024*. CP Group Global, 2024, cpgroupglobal.com/storage/document/sustainability-reports/2024/sustainability-report-2024-en.pdf.
9. "Emirates Fleet Details and History." *Planespotters*, 2025, planespotters.net/airline/Emirates.
10. "Our Fleet | The Emirates Experience." *Emirates*, emirates.com/ca/english/experience/our-fleet/.
11. Media Center, "Emirates Joins IATA's Turbulence Aware Platform, Becomes First Airline to Integrate Flight Data for Real-Time Accuracy with Lido mPilot from Lufthansa Systems." *Emirates*, 2024, emirates.com/media-centre/emirates-joins-iatas-turbulence-aware-platform-becomes-first-airline-to-integrate-flight-data-for-real-time-accuracy-with-lido-mpilot-from-lufthansa-systems/.
12. "Understanding the I Ching: The Ancient Chinese Book of Changes." *Selfgazer*, selfgazer.com/blog/what-is-the-iching.
13. "Who We Are." *Tata Consultancy Services*, tcs.com/who-we-are.
14. "TCS HOBS for Context-Driven Engagement." *Tata Consultancy Services*, tcs.com/what-we-do/products-platforms/tcs-hobs/solution/hobs-for-context-driven-engagement.
15. Lee, Seung-Woo. "Naver Aims to Attract 1 bn Users via Active M&As by 2027." *The Korea Economic Daily Global Edition*, 2022, kedglobal.com/tech,-media-telecom/newsView/ked202204130019.

16. Evertiq, "LS Electric Partners with Naver on AI-Based Power, Data Center Solutions." *Evertiq*, 2025, evertiq.com/design/2025-08-01-ls-electric-partners-with-naver-on-ai-based-power-data-center-solutions.
17. "What Is Tiered Data Storage?" *Pure Storage*, purestorage.com/knowledge/what-is-tiered-data-storage.html.
18. Shirley Fernandes, "An Overview of Siheyuan." *Rethinking The Future*, re-thinkingthefuture.com/architectural-styles/a5900-an-overview-of-siheyuan/.
19. Butler, Georgia. "Alibaba Cloud Reaffirms $52.7bn Global Buildout Plans." *Data Center Dynamics*, 2025, datacenterdynamics.com/en/news/alibaba-cloud-reaffirms-527bn-global-buildout-plans/.
20. Zhang, Jane. "How Alibaba Powered Billions of Transactions on Singles' Day with 'Zero Downtime'." *South China Morning Post*, 2019, scmp.com/tech/e-commerce/article/3038539/how-alibaba-powered-billions-transactions-singles-day-zero-downtime.
21. "Flann Gao, Luica Mak, Alibaba Cloud Powered $1B of GMV in 68 Seconds, with Zero Downtime During 11.11." *Alibaba Cloud*, 2019, alibabacloud.com/en/press-room/alibaba-cloud-powered-1b-of-gmv-in-68-seconds?_p_lc=1.
22. Chen, Jidong, et al. "Big Data Based Fraud Risk Management at Alibaba." *ScienceDirect*, 2015, sciencedirect.com/science/article/pii/S2405918815000021.
23. "The Analects: Xue Er." *Chinese Text Project*, translated by James Legge, ctext.org/analects/xue-er.
24. Tang, Alan, et al. "AI for Public Good: From Vision to Action and Innovation." *United Nations Development Programme*, 2025, undp.org/policy-centre/singapore/blog/ai-public-good-vision-action-and-innovation.
25. Singapore News Centre. "GovTech's LaunchPad Ignites AI Innovation across Singapore's Public Sector." *Microsoft Source*, 2024, news.microsoft.com/en-sg/2024/04/25/govtechs-launchpad-ignites-ai-innovation-across-singapores-public-sector/.
26. Ping An Insurance (Group) Company of China, Ltd. "Ping An Reports Stable Operating Profit Attributable to Shareholders of the Parent Company and Interim Dividends, with a 6.8% YoY Increase in Net Profit." *PR Newswire*, 2024, prnewswire.com/news-releases/ping-an-reports-stable-operating-profit-attributable-to-shareholders-of-the-parent-company-and-interim-dividends-with-a-6-8-yoy-increase-in-net-profit-302228542.html.
27. "About Us." *Ping An*, group.pingan.com/about_us.html.
28. Stefon, Matt. "Junzi." *Encyclopedia Britannica*, 2016, britannica.com/topic/junzi.
29. Translation of 以文化人. *Reverso Context*, context.reverso.net/%E7%BF%BB%E8%AF%91/%E4%B8%AD%E6%96%87-%E8%8B%B1%E8%AF%AD/%E4%BB%A5%E6%96%87%E5%8C%96%E4%BA%BA.
30. LG Electronics. "LG Presents Vision to 'Reinvent Your Future' with AI-Powered Innovations at LG World Premiere." *It Web*, 2024, itweb.

co.za/article/lg-presents-vision-to-reinvent-your-future-with-ai-powered-innovations-at-lg-world-premiere/LPp6VMrB352MDKQz.

31. 亚洲法律杂志. "Singapore Leads with Principles-Based Approach to AI in Financial Services." *Asian Legal Business*, 2024, legalbusinessonline.com/features/singapore-leads-principles-based-approach-ai-financial-services.
32. Kyung-min, Lee. "KB Financial Establishes Digital Innovation Department to Accelerate AI Drive." *The Korea Times*, 2025, koreatimes.co.kr/economy/20250701/kb-financial-establishes-digital-innovation-department-to-accelerate-ai-drive.
33. "Commonwealth Bank Of Australia: Number of Employees 2020-2024 | CMWAY." *Macrotrends*, 2024, macrotrends.net/stocks/charts/CMWAY/commonwealth-bank-of-australia/number-of-employees.
34. "Artificial Intelligence." *Commonwealth Bank of Australia*, commbank.com.au/about-us/opportunity-initiatives/policies-and-practices/artificial-intelligence.html.
35. Gargano, Frank. "RBC Rolls Out AI-Based Tools to Financial Advisors." *American Banker*, 2024, americanbanker.com/news/rbc-rolls-out-ai-based-tools-to-financial-advisors.
36. "Responsible AI." *Rakuten*, global.rakuten.com/corp/sustainability/ResponsibleAI/.
37. "Complete Guide to Bias Bounty Programs: Building Ethical AI Systems." *Troy Lendman*, troylendman.com/complete-guide-to-bias-bounty-programs-building-ethical-ai-systems/.
38. Yaseen, Hadeel, and Asma'a Al-Amarneh. "Adoption of Artificial Intelligence-Driven Fraud Detection in Banking: The Role of Trust, Transparency, and Fairness Perception in Financial Institutions in the United Arab Emirates and Qatar." *Multidisciplinary Digital Publishing Institute*, 2025, mdpi.com/1911-8074/18/4/217.

CHAPTER 3

Finding High-Impact AI Use Cases

Beyond the Hype

Sun Tzu teaches in *The Art of War* to "know yourself and know your enemy."[1] This principle applies perfectly to AI adoption. Instead of getting distracted by every new AI tool, identify which applications will truly boost your competitive edge.

This chapter gives you proven strategies to:

1. **Separate winners from time-wasters:** Our scoring system helps you evaluate AI projects based on business impact, not just popularity and technical gaudiness.
2. **Learn from real success stories:** We break down the different ways industry leaders are using AI with concrete results you can replicate.
3. **Avoid costly mistakes:** Learn the top reasons AI projects fail (hint: it's usually not the technology's fault) and how to sidestep these issues.
4. **Calculate the real ROI:** Move beyond the hype with our practical tools for measuring actual returns, including hidden costs and benefits you might be missing.

The most effective AI strategies borrow from timeless principles. Play into your organization's unique strengths; enhance rather than disrupt

DOI: 10.1201/9781003644699-3

existing workflows; bypass current trends; and focus on solutions that make the most sense for *you*. At the end of day, successful AI adoption is all about making smart choices that drive meaningful results. This chapter shows you how.

SECTION 1: STRUCTURED AI OPPORTUNITY ASSESSMENT

Today's AI landscape is more misleading than ever. From chatbots pulling "facts" out of thin air to predictive analytics claiming to forecast the next quarter's profits, how do you separate the game changers from the gimmicks? With so many AI tools out there, the key is to take a structured approach, balancing risks, costs, and long-term impact before committing to a solution.

The real challenge isn't finding an AI opportunity; there are plenty out there. The difficult part is to figure out which ones are worth pursuing. Without a clear way to assess them, companies often end up chasing the wrong projects or underestimating what it takes to make them work. That's why a methodical evaluation process, one that starts with careful planning and stays grounded in real-world applications, is crucial.

1.1 THE FOUR PILLARS OF AI OPPORTUNITY EVALUATION

Choosing the right AI projects is about weighing four key factors together:

1. **Business impact potential** (will this actually move the needle?)
2. **Implementation feasibility** (can we realistically make this work?)
3. **Organizational readiness** (do we have the skills and data to succeed?)
4. **Strategic alignment** (does this fit into where we are going as a company?)

These four pillars are interconnected. For example, a project might look great on paper with high-impact, but if your team lacks the right data or the idea doesn't align with long-term goals, it could end up as wasted effort. All four factors need to be evaluated together for the best results.

1.1.1 Business Impact Potential: Measuring What Really Matters

When evaluating an AI opportunity, the first question should always be: how will this create real, measurable value for our business? Here is a five-point stress test with the key impact categories you can use to help spot real business value for your organization. For each impact category, ask these make-or-break questions upfront:

1. **Revenue potential:**
   - Will customers actually pay more for this?
   - Can this unlock new markets or premium pricing?
2. **Cost reduction:**
   - What percentage of inefficiency will this eliminate?
   - Does this automate labor-intensive tasks?
3. **Risk mitigation:**
   - How much compliance risk does this remove?
   - Will this prevent costly privacy complications?
4. **Competitive differentiation:**
   - Is this something competitors can easily copy?
   - Does this open up unique possibilities?
5. **Scalability:**
   - How can we 10× this across the business?
   - Does this create reusable intellectual property?

Once you have defined the category and the right questions to ask, allocate points across these categories. For example, use a 0–100 scoring scale across revenue (30 points), cost (25 points), risk (20 points), uniqueness (15 points), and scalability (10 points). But remember that the weighting shown here is illustrative; your organization should distribute points in a way that reflects your unique risk tolerance and strategic goals. A weighted scoring system helps companies assess opportunities objectively and consistently across multiple use cases.

1.1.2 Implementation Feasibility: Working With Reality, Not Against It

Before committing to an AI initiative, smart teams ask one crucial question: "Does this fit our current reality?" That's where the feasibility assessment comes in. It evaluates the following four critical dimensions:

1. **Technical compatibility:** Alignment with existing systems and infrastructure. Asking key questions like "are pre-trained models available, or must we build from scratch?"; "how many existing systems must this connect to (CRM, ERP, etc.)?"; "Can our current cloud handle the compute load? What are the processing demands?"
2. **Resource availability:** Budget, personnel, and time allocations. Considering: "Is this project fully funded or are we banking on future approvals?"; "Do we have in-house AI/ML engineers, or will we need to hire contractors?"; "Are other departments competing for the same resources?"
3. **Operational constraints:** Realistic timelines and manageable dependencies. Your questions should sound something like "Is this timeline based on similar past projects, or an optimistic guess?"; "Are we waiting on third-party vendors for critical components?"
4. **Strategic fit:** Alignment with short-term roadmaps and long-term visions. "Is this timed to support a critical business milestone (product launch, etc.)?"; "Does this address a pain point for customers/partners?"; "Will this solution scale with our plans for growth?"

The key is to work with your current strengths *and* limitations. That means being brutally honest about what's truly possible with what you have today, rather than banking on hypothetical future improvements. For example, an advanced predictive analytics model may promise impressive outcomes, but if it requires infrastructure upgrades beyond current IT roadmaps, a simpler initial solution is ultimately more effective.

1.1.3 Organizational Readiness: Is Your Company Truly Prepared for AI?

As we explored in depth in Chapter 2, AI success depends far more on organizational factors than purely technical ones. AI thrives based on your company's culture, leadership, and ability to adapt. The same technology that thrives in one company can flop in another simply due to differences in executive buy-in, change management, and workforce readiness, as we've seen play out across various case studies.

Here is how to assess whether or not your organization is prepared for AI, building on the frameworks we established earlier:

1. **Leadership commitment:** Do executives actively champion AI, or is it just another IT project to them? Are budgets and resources allocated upfront, or is funding vague? Is AI tied to strategic goals (e.g. customer experience, efficiency), or is it just an attempt to flaunt innovation? These questions will help catch any red flags; for example if leadership views AI as a nice-to-have rather than a must-win, adoption will likely stall rather than support the rest of your business.

2. **Culture**: These questions will help find out whether your company collectively embraces change or resists it: how do employees react to new tech? Is failure treated as a learning opportunity or a career risk? Does innovation happen organically, or does every change feel like pulling teeth? Hint: companies that fundamentally encourage learning adopt AI far more successfully.

3. **Change management:** Building on the model established in Chapter 2, ask the following questions: does your company have a track record of successful digital transformation? Are there clear processes in place for training, communication, and feedback exchange? Who is responsible for driving adoption? Would it be IT, business units, or a dedicated AI team? If past tech rollouts have been chaotic, implementing AI will entail the same hurdles.

4. **Stakeholder alignment:** This helps identify who is on board. Asking: do frontline employees see AI as an aid or a threat? Are key departments aligned on priorities? For every impacted team, is there a clear "what's in it for me?" Run focus groups with end users early on, as misalignment kills more AI projects than bad algorithms.

Here we are reinforcing Chapter 2's central thesis that AI readiness is as much about the people, process, and leadership as it is about the technology.

1.1.4 Strategic Alignment: Creating Long-Term Value

Goal alignment ensures that your AI investments reinforce your competitiveness, rather than simply solving technical problems. The first step is to identify the core areas that already give your company a unique competitive edge; then value each factor by asking some key questions. Provided below is an example of a playbook for strategic AI, using Alibaba's case study:

1. **Ecosystem reinforcement:** The key question to ask is, "does this strategy help make our partners/suppliers/customers more successful?" For example, Alibaba's AI-powered inventory forecasting system benefits both merchants and logistics partners, helping on both ends of the process by predicting demand and thus optimizing inventory placement.[2]
2. **Platform effects:** "Will this make our platform more valuable as an increasing number of people begin to use it?" Alibaba's recommendation AI learns from and gets smarter with each purchase, locking in user loyalty as they can increasingly rely on its suggestions.
3. **Moat deepening:** "Does this advantage compound over time?" Alibaba is a strong example of this. Their cloud AI services become stickier as clients build on them.

The best AI initiatives check multiple boxes. In Alibaba's case, their logistics AI strengthens their ecosystem, platform, and data advantages simultaneously.

1.2 INTEGRATED SCORING METHODOLOGY

A repeat of what we discussed previously, the right choice for your AI project comes down to carefully weighting four key factors together: business impact (will this actually matter?), feasibility (can we pull it off?), organizational readiness (are we set up for success?), and strategic fit (does this align with where we want to be?).

We now know what to evaluate for in each factor and the key questions to ask. But with dozens of potential projects on the table, we need one crucial final piece: a simple but effective scoring system to objectively compare options and invest in the right ones.

1.2.1 The Four-Pillar Scorecard

Below is a sample scorecard (see Table 3.1). Adjust the weights based on your organization's priorities. For example, if you are risk-averse, bump up feasibility; if you are playing to maintain your wins in the long term, boost strategic fit; and if your business is in turnaround mode, prioritize business impact.

Optionally, you may add time constraints as well. For example, if results can be achieved within the year, then assign full points, while only giving 80% credit if the timeline extends to three years.

1.2.2 How Scoring Works in Practice

1. Assemble a diverse team: Schedule for the technical, strategic, and business leaders to work together. Avoid scoring in silos.
2. Score independently, then debate: Have individuals rate each pillar (1–100) and then discuss discrepancies in opinion. For instance, why technical teams think implementation will be simple while operations say it's not possible?
3. Consensus beats technical perfection: Settle on one score per pillar that is generally agreed on, rather than taking averages.

1.2.3 Decision Thresholds (Customisable)

- >80 points: Green light. Project should go full steam ahead
- 60–79 points: Fix weaknesses or stage a pilot run
- <40 points: Rebuild or reject

Keep in mind that some companies reserve 10% of their budget for those projects with under 40 points, such as Amazon's Alexa, which initially was believed to be a long shot.[3]

TABLE 3.1 Illustrating The Four-Pillar Scorecard

Pillar	Weight (%)	What It Measures
Business impact	40	Revenue, cost savings, competitive edge
Feasibility	25	Tech, data, and resource realities
Organizational readiness	20	Culture, leadership, and change capacity
Strategic fit	15	Alignment with long-term goals

SECTION 2: INDUSTRY-SPECIFIC AI APPLICATIONS

The most transformative AI applications today are those built for vertical markets, solving problems that general-purpose models can't address.

In healthcare, for example, although AI has been widely implemented, what's truly saving lives is AI applications for critical ill care, where systems analyze electronic health record data in real time and send alerts when a patient's condition deteriorates. Similar successes can be seen across the manufacturing, financial, and retail industries. We will continue to analyze the successful use cases of each of these industries in this section.

These successes share a common theme: AI must be programmed into industry DNA, with algorithms trained on domain-specific data, must be designed to impact real workflows, and must be measured by business outcomes. The future belongs to companies that invest in deep vertical solutions.

2.1 MANUFACTURING EXCELLENCE THROUGH PREDICTIVE INTELLIGENCE

Japan's FANUC Corporation is one of the world's leading manufacturers in industrial automation and robotics, famous for its bright yellow factory robots. While most tech companies try to force generic AI into factories, FANUC is changing the game by building solutions that speak manufacturing's unique language. Here is why their approach is successful.

2.1.1 They Solve Problems Only Manufacturers Understand

FANUC's AI goes beyond generic predictions by addressing nuanced manufacturing challenges, such as the following:

1. Material-specific tool wear and tear. Their adaptive AI machining system is able to account for how aluminum (soft metal) causes different tool degradation patterns compared to titanium (tougher metal).[4]
2. Industry-tailored vibration analyses. They recognized that vibration patterns matter more in automotive plants than in electronics and adjusted their approach accordingly. For example, focusing on high-frequency vibrations from stamping presses in automotive plants, and instead prioritizing micro-vibrations in printed circuit board (PCB) assembly.[5]

3. Environmental compensation. As temperature and humidity fluctuations affect precision in different production environments, their smart system automatically adjusts for thermal expansion in part machining, where even a 0.001-inch difference matters.[6]

2.1.2 Why Competitors Are Unable to Copy This

By focusing on industry-specific details and embedding AI directly into their assembly line, FANUC created the following:

1. Data moats: They leverage their refined algorithms for tool wear, thermal drift, and process stability, creating a self-reinforcing competitive edge.
2. Additional loops: Manufacturing plants using FANUC's systems can't switch without significantly hindering efficiency.
3. Compound intelligence: Each factory's learnings reinforce that of every other team.

FANUC proves that AI triumphs in manufacturing when it is built by people who truly understand manufacturing. Their algorithms are trained on real machine shop problems and are integrated into the tools workers already use. While Silicon Valley sells AI that could work anywhere, FANUC focuses solely on building what works in manufacturing—and that is why they dominate.

2.2 TRANSFORMING HEALTHCARE THROUGH CLINICAL INTELLIGENCE

India has a very complex healthcare landscape, where 1.4 billion people face vast disparities in accessibility and resources. Apollo Hospitals has found a way to make AI work in healthcare. Instead of using mass-produced, generalized AI tools, they built solutions that only work for India's unique healthcare challenges. This is what has made them so successful. Here is the inside story.

2.2.1 They Solve Problems Only Applicable to Indian Doctors

What sets Apollo apart is that their algorithms are trained on extensive and diverse datasets within their clinic databases to identify and resolve the following:

1. Regional disease patterns: Trained on local data, their AI is able to recognize that certain ailments progress significantly faster in specific areas due to regional dietary patterns.[7]

2. Local resource constraints: Only treatments that are available at rural clinics, and medicine that is actually stocked at district hospitals, are recommended. Treatment plans can also be adjusted to accommodate frequent power outages.[8]

3. Population-specific risks: In its recommendations, their algorithms account for genetic and lifestyle factors common in Indian patients.

2.2.2 Why Competitors Can't Catch Up

Apollo has an unbeatable data advantage that is not easily replicated:

- The data flywheel effect: Apollo has approximately 4 million annual patient encounters,[9] spanning diverse demographics across India. By combining their extensive clinical database with their advanced AI capabilities, they create a self-reinforcing data flywheel where more patient volume generates more data that feeds into their AI engine.
- The impenetrable moat: For others to catch up, they will require a minimum of ten years' worth of data specific to India in order to match Apollo's current level of accuracy. With their extensive network of academic partnerships, including collaborations with several prestigious scientific institutions, the bar has been set very high.[10]

2.3 FINANCIAL SERVICE INNOVATION THROUGH RISK INTELLIGENCE

Brazil is seen as an emerging market by banks around the world. Itaú Unibanco interacts with up to 100 million unique customer financial profiles.[11] Itaú has built AI solutions to match this vision; this has brought them unbeatable competitive advantages.

2.3.1 Cracking Brazil's Toughest Financial Puzzles

Itaú's AI can adeptly assess risks, just like many other banks with similar values. But what sets their system apart is that it also has the built-in capability to handle Brazil's unique financial landscape.

1. Providing credit for the informal economy: For the portion of the population that don't go to the bank, Itaú assesses risks by analyzing utility payment histories and other similar transactions.[12]

2. Putting in place a fraud shield: When Brazil launched its Pix instant payment system, fraudsters brought out their own gold rush through fake invoice scams, small "test thefts" before big hits, and impersonating bank agents. Standard fraud systems are unable to recognize the style of new Portuguese scam calls and miss cultural context. Itaú localized their defense system by setting local language AI traps (such as flagging voice patterns in call centers) and doing real-time analysis through mapping scammer networks in order to freeze funds before withdrawals.[13]

3. Implementing regulatory autopilot: Brazil's financial regulations are highly dynamic and subject to change. While most banks throw teams of lawyers at the problem, Itaú automatically updates their systems with the latest changes, cutting compliance costs.[14]

2.3.2 Why Global Banks Can't Compete

Itaú has fully leveraged its home-field advantage with (a) multiple years of Brazil-specific transaction data, and (b) a strong understanding of local fraud patterns.

Itaú's success proves that financial AI is able to succeed when it is built for local financial habits, trained on regional threats, and programmed with country-specific regulations.

2.4 RETAIL EVOLUTION THROUGH CUSTOMER INTELLIGENCE

JD.com builds their every algorithm specifically for China's complex commerce challenges that are unable to be solved by generic retail AI. Here is how they created this unique competitive advantage by packing deep localization into the solution.

2.4.1 Solving China-Scale Retail Problems

Conquering China's "last-mile" puzzle: JD.com has tailored its logistics AI to address both urban and rural challenges. In cities, its algorithms navigate traffic congestion and complex apartment access systems, while in rural areas, AI optimizes village pickup points and farm-to-market coordination. This dual approach supports JD's ability to achieve up to 95% same-day or next-day delivery across China. It's an industry-leading rate that outperforms competitors across the board.[15]

China's retail market spans vastly different climates and cuisines, creating enormous difficulties in stock management. JD meets these challenges by running one of the world's largest product catalogs, with over 5 million SKUs as of 2020 (compared to Walmart, which has fewer than 30,000).[16] This unprecedented scale is powered by AI-driven logistics and demand forecasting, allowing JD to adapt inventory flows to local needs while keeping fulfillment efficient.

Regional fragmentation makes China's retail one of the hardest to navigate in the world; what sells in Shanghai may not sell in Chengdu, and demand changes by the hour. JD addresses this through its 7Fresh grocery platform, where its AI system was able to boost full order fulfillment rates by 4.3% over traditional methods,[17] showing how localized demand forecasting can keep shelves stocked and customers satisfied, even in a fragmented market.

JD's winning formula entails engineering AI exclusively for China's retail complexity. Their 100%-owned logistics data ensures that there are no third-party blind spots. Fifteen years of China-specific purchase patterns and accurate location mapping make it very hard for competitors to copy.[18]

2.5 EMERGING SECTOR OPPORTUNITIES THROUGH ADAPTIVE INTELLIGENCE

In emerging sectors, smart companies are finding opportunities that stretch far vertically as well. Samsung SDI, the world's second-largest EV battery maker, has created unique advantages for itself by speaking industry-specific language fluently. For example, with their climate-adaptive batteries, all global battery manufacturers struggle with performance variance across climates, which affects battery life. Similar to FANUC's thermal displacement compensation technology, Samsung SDI's AI solution adjusts charging for extreme weather conditions, allowing for operation in temperatures ranging from –20 to –60°C, and preventing material corrosion when in a humid environment.[19]

Emerging markets demand tailored AI. While Seoul-specific solutions may fail in São Paulo, hyper-local systems thrive by building vertical AI systems for exact local needs and letting real-world problems guide development.

SECTION 3: COMMON AI IMPLEMENTATION PITFALLS

Sun Tzu's warning that "all warfare is based on deception" applies perfectly to AI implementations today, as hidden pitfalls often derail the best-founded initiatives. Across industries, companies keep making the same mistakes: chasing cutting-edge AI without solving truly impactful business problems, assuming that their data and workforce are both up to speed.

In this section, we will discuss the five most common reasons AI projects fail, and how spotting these traps early on can turn potential disasters into competitive advantages.

3.1 WHEN OVERPROMISING LEADS TO UNDERDELIVERING

The fastest way to kill an AI project? Falling into the trap of believing that AI will solve your every problem instantly, when in reality, even the most advanced systems have limitations and require careful implementation.

China's tech conglomerate LeEco proved this painfully. LeEco started off as China's Netflix, before expanding into TVs, phones, and grand promises of self-driving AI cars by 2020. Its ambitions quickly died after hitting technical and regulatory walls, and they eventually collapsed in 2017.[20] LeEco stands as a textbook case of how AI hype without proper thought and execution leads to disaster.

A pattern emerges from similar failures:

- The mirage of instant perfection: Expecting 100% accuracy from day one, when in reality, progress always hits the "last 10% problem" where improvements and motivation slow dramatically.
- Underestimating the grind: The average AI project takes 18–24 months to mature.[21] Expecting grand automation in a short period of time often leads to failure.
- Probability vs. promises: AI gives likely answers, not guarantees. Not being able to recognize AI's limitations leads to inevitable challenges down the road.

Unrealistic expectations remain the leading cause of AI implementation failures, as organizations routinely overestimate their capabilities while ignoring operational requirements and technological limitations. Companies that choose to set incremental milestones and measure progress in small, concrete wins see more consistent success toward building larger AI ambitions.

3.2 BAD DATA: THE DIRTY SECRET OF AI FAILURE

Poor data remains AI's most preventable failure point. While technical challenges get all the attention, discrepancies in data quality, completeness, and relevance often are the cause of failure for even the most advanced AI systems. As India's healthcare sector shows, 2 in 3 AI projects fail before launch, with the main cause being data fragmentation.[22]

Here is how to prepare and get on top of the issue:

1. The "sharpen your tools" principle: Like craftsmen sharpening tools before carving, successful AI teams prioritize data cleaning before modeling.
2. Future-proof your data: Build governance for privacy compliance (GDPR, HIPAA, etc.) and make sure that what is built is reusable across multiple AI projects.
3. The sustainability mindset: Treat data preparation as an ongoing hygiene step, and not a one-time effort. Furthermore, monitor and record changes in data (requirements, patterns, completeness) over time. What works for you in 2025 may no longer be sufficient in 2030.

Smart teams invest most of their AI effort (>60%) in bulletproofing data upfront, avoiding the performance issues and broken trust that come with cutting corners in data quality.

3.3 POOR STAKEHOLDER ENGAGEMENT: THE HUMAN FACTOR IN TECHNICAL FAILURE

Time and time again, technically brilliant AI projects fail because teams did not bring stakeholders along for the journey. Either employees resist it, managers distrust it, or customers reject it, simply because management solves perceived problems instead of real user needs.

The Confucian principle of "harmony through difference (和而不同)" offers a blueprint for AI adoption. Success comes from the ability to align on common goals despite the fact that different stakeholder groups may have diverse viewpoints. Companies that co-design AI with users (not merely for them) see significantly higher adoption rates.[23]

Effective engagement often means considering both logic ("how will this work?") and emotions ("will this replace my role?"). Through open, transparent, and consistent communication, long-lasting trust can be built against AI resistance.

3.4 INSUFFICIENT CHANGE MANAGEMENT: WHY YOUR AI IS FAILING

The number 1 reason AI projects fail in reality has nothing to do with technology. On the contrary, it's the human side of things that gets ignored. A surprisingly large chunk of AI failures stem from poor change management. In reality, success is only 10% dependent on the technology, and 70% reliant on the people involved.[24] When companies roll out AI without updating how people work, measure success, or make decisions, they end up with expensive systems collecting dust because they never learned to use them.

These statistics show us that AI delivers real results only when companies redesign both workflows *and* rewards. Addressing the change management gap is a step that many organizations need to take in order to fully take advantage of what technology brings to the table.

SECTION 4: CALCULATING AI PROJECT ROI—THE PRACTICAL FRAMEWORK TO MEASURE AI's REAL BUSINESS IMPACT

Evaluating AI projects effectively goes beyond simple cost–benefit analysis. Organizations need to look at both tangible benefits and hard-to-measure long-term advantages. Those are the factors often overlooked by traditional ROI calculations.

The key lies in making decisions based on factual evidence, not optimistic projections. By honestly and realistically assessing costs, timelines, and strategic fit, businesses can make smarter investment decisions that deliver lasting value.

4.1 THE LIMITATION OF TRADITIONAL ROI MODELS FOR AI PROJECTS

Traditional ROI calculations rely on linear assumptions regarding costs, timelines, and risks. These factors behave very differently in AI projects compared to conventional IT investments. For example, when manufacturers such as Coca-Cola utilize Aquant's AI-driven predictive maintenance, traditional ROI models fall short. Although these models assume straightforward cost savings, the actual gains emerge over time: service costs drop by up to 23% annually, unexpected downtime falls sharply, and operational efficiency improves.[25] These benefits compound and only become visible after deployment matures, which mainstream ROI models miss, because they don't take into account evolving benefits post-launch.

Unlike traditional tech projects, AI delivers value in non-linear ways. Early stages may show minimal returns as models train and improve. Then, the benefits begin to grow rapidly as the system matures. This process is similar to cultivating a tree, which takes patience and faith before yielding results.

4.2 ASSESSMENT FRAMEWORK

Below is a straightforward, business-friendly approach to capture what is needed for accurate ROI calculation.

4.2.1 Measure What Matters: The Visible Benefits

Track concrete improvement, such as the following:

- Cost savings (e.g. reduced manual work, lower error rates)
- Revenue growth (increased sales from AI-powered recommendations)
- Productivity gains (faster processing times)

Example: A bank using AI fraud detection to significantly cut the amount of false alarms they get, saving a significant portion of funds annually while improving customer experience.

4.2.2 Don't Miss the Hidden Wins

Some of AI's biggest payoffs are more difficult to measure but are just as important to note:

- Faster, better decision-making (predictive analytics accelerating planning)
- Stronger workforce capabilities (employees solving problems faster with AI assistants)
- Unlocking new opportunities (spotting trends that lead to innovative products)

Example: An automaker reducing vehicle development time by 25% using AI design tools, achieving far beyond their original cost-saving goals.

4.2.3 Budget for the Real Costs

Consider the following factors, which often cause AI projects to exceed initial cost estimates:

- Data cleanup and preparation (takes up a significant portion of project time)
- Employee training and adoption (6–12 months for full productivity)
- Ongoing maintenance (AI models need regular updates)

Example: A quality control AI system with a $1.6M budget that balloons to $3.4M, yet still delivering 229% ROI by year three through defect reduction.

4.2.4 Plan for the Inevitable Risks

Every AI project faces challenges that need to be managed proactively:

- Implementation hurdles (data quality issues delaying launch dates)
- Adoption resistance (teams needing change management support)
- Setting realistic timelines (the time it takes for AI optimization to surpass human planners)

Example: A European retailer's AI inventory system initially underperforming due to legacy data gaps, requiring four extra months of cleaning but ultimately reducing stockout by 28%.

4.3 AI PROJECT ROI CALCULATION: FROM THEORY TO PRACTICE

Building on the framework we developed in this chapter, here is a simple method that helps you capture the full value of AI, including both quantifiable benefits, and hard-to-measure long-term advantages to help make better decisions and introduce new AI capabilities (Table 3.2). Full spectrum cost and risk planning are also built in to take into consideration hidden factors that can potentially derail your AI projects.

4.3.1 A Practical Method to Measure What Matters

TABLE 3.2 Measure What Matters

Feature	What It Does	Why It Matters
Benefit quantifier	Tracks both direct savings (e.g. 25% operation costs) and indirect value (e.g. faster decision-making)	Avoids undervaluing projects
Cost reality check	Includes often-missed items such as data prep and change management	Prevents budget overruns
Risk simulator	Models three scenarios (best-case, worst-case, most likely)	Shows true risk/reward
Timeline mapper	Accounts for AI's learning curve (e.g. 6–12 month adoption)	Sets realistic and measurable expectations

TABLE 3.3 Measure What Matters—Example

Metric	Before AI	Year 1	Year 3
Defect rate (%)	8	5	2
Maintenance costs	$1.2M	$0.9M	$0.6M
New products launched	2/year	3/year	5/year

4.3.2 How It Works in Practice

1. Input your baseline (current metrics, costs)
2. Customize variables (improvement targets, timeline)
3. Run scenarios (test different assumptions)
4. Get actionable insights (break-even point projection, total value potential, key risk factors)

Table 3.3 provides a hypothetical example drown from a manufacturing client.

4.3.3 Implementation Roadmap

Unlike with traditional software, AI gets gradually smarter but will need some time to ramp up. Plan for the following:

- A pilot phase (3–6 months) in order to validate assumptions
- A scale phase (6–18 months) for monitoring real-world results
- An optimization phase (ongoing) to account for continuous improvement beyond launch

This framework provides organizations with a measurable roadmap to put toward their AI investments, using evidence-based strategy.

4.4 ADVANCED ROI CONSIDERATIONS FOR AI PROJECTS

We have covered the fundamentals of AI ROI calculation in previous sections; here we look further. There are three transformative dimensions that go beyond traditional project boundaries:

1. Network effects: AI creates a ripple effect across teams through:
   - Cross-functional decision-making (e.g. supply chain AI improving finance forecasting)

- Organizational learning (diagnostic AI helping radiologists train junior staff)
- Improved collaboration (chatbots reducing IT tickets while improving employee experience)

2. Scalability potential: Planning for growth from day one. When implementing AI, ask yourself, "where else could this AI work; what's the expansion roadmap?" Scalability drastically improves results, as more data creates smarter AI which leads to better outcomes.

   Example: An AI system built to monitor crop yields at one farm is adapted to 50+ farms, spreading development cost across the entire network.

3. Future-proofing your business: Often, these AI projects create long-term benefits beyond immediate financial returns:

   - Talent magnetism (top engineers flock to AI-forward companies)
   - Additional value (today's cost saver becomes tomorrow's new product platform)

   Planning principle: like chess masters, the best AI investors think three moves ahead!

These additional dimensions show that smart AI investments deliver more than just immediate financial returns but also position organizations for long-term opportunities and challenges.

4.5 BEST PRACTICES FOR MAXIMIZING AI ROI

To turn AI investments into lasting business results, follow these proven approaches:

1. Start small, scale smart

   - Pilot with clear success metrics (e.g. "we aim to reduce customer service response time by 30% in 3 months")
   - Plan expansion only after proving initial value (e.g. a retailer testing AI inventory management in ten stores before rolling it out nationwide.)

2. Track progress relentlessly and adjust actions accordingly

   Set clear checkpoints to monitor progress and realign goals if needed. For example,

   - Monthly: Are we on track technically? (e.g. if missing more than two milestones, reallocate resources)
   - Quarterly: Is ROI meeting our projections?
   - Bi-Annually: Does this still align with our strategy?

   Example: A logistics company's AI routing project is found to be underperforming during their Q1 review. By reallocating three engineers to fix data issues and adding customer delivery feedback, the failing pilot quickly became a profitable ROI solution.

3. Build on real-world learning

   - Document what works and what doesn't through a SWOT analysis
   - Adjust ROI models based on actual performance data

4. Prepare for evolution

   - Set aside a budget for model updates
   - Plan for employee skill development

SECTION 5: FROM STRATEGIC SELECTION TO SYSTEMATIC IMPLEMENTATION

This chapter has provided practical frameworks to help organizations identify high-impact AI use cases that deliver real business value. By focusing on business impact potential, implementation feasibility, organizational readiness, and alignment with long-term objectives, leaders can avoid costly missteps and prioritize initiatives that can genuinely transform their business.

However, selecting the right AI projects is only the beginning. Research from MIT reveals that 95% of AI initiatives fail to deliver measurable returns.[26] Common reasons include inadequate data preparation, collective resistance to change, and difficulty integrating with legacy systems.

As we look ahead, Chapter 4 will provide the practical playbook for bridging this implementation gap. The journey to operational excellence separates those experimenting with AI from those that are looking to transform their businesses.

NOTES

1. Sun Tzu, *The Art of War. The Internet Classics Archive*, translated by Lionel Gates, classics.mit.edu/Tzu/artwar.html.
2. Alizila Staff. "At Alibaba, Artificial Intelligence is Changing How People Shop Online." *Alizila*, 2017, alizila.com/at-alibaba-artificial-intelligence-is-changing-how-people-shop-online/.
3. Hartmans, Avery, and Grace Kay. "Amazon Trained Alexa in Secret by Hiring Unsuspecting People to Ask Questions in a Room Filled with Hidden Prototypes." *Business Insider*, 2021, businessinsider.com/how-amazon-created-alexa-trained-echo-while-keeping-secret-2021-5.
4. "New Function: Cutting Load Monitor Function." *FANUC*, 2022, fanuc.co.jp/en/product/new_product/2022/202206_cuttingloadmonitor.html.
5. Chen, Juan, et al. "Micro-Vibration Measurement and Analysis of High-Tech Electronics Workshop in Guangzhou." *Springer Nature Link*, 2017, link.springer.com/chapter/10.1007/978-981-10-4508-0_24. "System and Method for Monitoring Operation of a Press Assembly." *Google Patents*, 2007, patents.google.com/patent/US20080178676A1/en.
6. "Thermal Displacement Compensation Software Functions." *FANUC Europe*, fanuc.eu/eu-en/eu-en/accessory/software/thermal-displacement-compensation-software-functions. "New Function: AI Thermal Displacement Compensation." *FANUC*, 2022, fanuc.co.jp/en/product/new_product/2022/202206_aithermaldisplacementcompensation.html.
7. Jha, Sneha. "Here's How Apollo Hospitals Is Leveraging AI to Predict Heart Disease." *Economic Times India*, 2018, cio.economictimes.indiatimes.com/news/strategy-and-management/heres-how-apollo-hospitals-is-leveraging-ai-to-predict-heart-disease/63874473.
8. "Innovative Use of Technology in Healthcare." *Apollo TeleHealth*, apollotelehealth.com/innovative-use-of-technology-in-healthcare/.
9. "Decarbonization through IT: GHG and Utility Inventory Platform." *Healthcare Climate Action*, 2025, healthcareclimateaction.org/CLI_Apollo-HospitalsGroup.
10. Dubey, Jayati. "Apollo Hospitals & University of Leicester Sign MoU for Global Healthcare Education & Research." *Digital Health News*, 2024, digitalhealthnews.com/apollo-hospitals-university-of-leicester-sign-mou-for-global-healthcare-education-research.
11. "Annual Integrated Report 2024." *Itaú Unibanco*, 2024, s2.q4cdn.com/476556808/files/doc_financials/2024/ar/ITCL_-Annual-Integrated-Report-2024_Itau-Chile_ENG.pdf.

12. Ferreira, Eduardo. "Itaú Unibanco: Banking the Unbanked in Brazil and the Value of Understanding People's Stories." *Inclusive Business*, 2015, https://endeva.org/wp-content/uploads/2015/08/bcta_casestudy_itau_web.pdf.
13. Woods, Audrey. "Case Study Itaú." *MIT Computer Science & Artificial Intelligence Laboratory*, cap.csail.mit.edu/sites/default/files/2025-01/Case%20Study%20Itau%20Edited%20%281%29.pdf.
14. Kitishian, Dany. "Itau Unibanco's AI Strategy: Analysis of Dominance in Banking AI." *Klover*, 2025, klover.ai/itau-unibanco-ai-strategy-analysis-of-dominance-in-banking-ai/.
15. Grant, Eli. "JD.com's Automation Gambit: A Blueprint for the Future of Retail and Logistics in China." *AI Invest*, 2025, ainvest.com/news/jd-automation-gambit-blueprint-future-retail-logistics-china-2507/.
16. "Alibaba vs JD.com: A Comparison of their 'Flywheel' Models." *Cheung Kong Graduate School of Business*, 2022, english.ckgsb.edu.cn/knowledge/article/alibaba-vs-jd-com-a-comparison-of-their-flywheel-models/.
17. Zhang, Zheming, et al. "OTPTO: Joint Product Selection and Inventory Optimization in Fresh E-commerce Front-End Warehouses." *arXiv*, 2025, arxiv.org/abs/2505.23421.
18. Biondi, Annachiara. "What the JD Logistics IPO Means for Luxury." *Vogue Business*, 2021, voguebusiness.com/consumers/jd-logistics-ipo-luxury-china.
19. "Why Choose Samsung SDI Lithium Batteries for Golf Cart Longevity?" *Redway Battery*, 2025, redwaybattery.com/why-choose-samsung-sdi-lithium-batteries-for-golf-cart-longevity/.
20. Yunxu, Qu. "2017 Sees Major Changes in China's Tech Landscape." *Caixin Global*, 2017, caixinglobal.com/2017-12-29/2017-sees-major-changes-in-chinas-tech-landscape-101191459.html.
21. Moorthy, Swathi. "Enterprises Will Take 18–24 Months to see Real Benefits of Agentic AI: IBM Executive." *Economic Times India*, 2025, economictimes.indiatimes.com/tech/artificial-intelligence/enterprises-will-take-18-24-months-to-see-real-benefits-of-agentic-ai-ibm-executive/articleshow/122582041.cms.
22. "India's AI Healthcare Revolution Is Stuck in Limbo—But New Infrastructure Could Change That." *Harcourt*, harcourthealth.com/indias-ai-healthcare-revolution-is-stuck-in-limbo-but-new-infrastructure-could-change-that/.
23. Bach, Tita Alissa, et al. "A Systematic Literature Review of User Trust in AI-Enabled Systems: An HCI Perspective." *arXiv*, 2023, arxiv.org/abs/2304.08795.
24. Persel, Ken. "The Hidden Leadership Gap Killing 70% of AI Transformations." *Medium*, 2025, medium.com/%40kenpersel21/the-hidden-leadership-gap-killing-70-of-ai-transformations-e4cecfc9b93c.
25. Mok, Aaron. "How AI and Robotics Can Help Prevent Breakdowns in Factories—and Save Manufacturers Big Bucks." *Business Insider*, 2025, businessinsider.com/artificial-intelligence-robotics-predictive-maintenance-manufacturing-factory-solutions-2025-5.

26. Morales, Jowi. "95% of Generative AI Implementations in Enterprise 'Have No Measurable Impact on P&L', Says MIT — Flawed Integration Cited As Why AI Projects Underperform." *Tom's Hardware*, 2025, tomshardware.com/tech-industry/artificial-intelligence/95-percent-of-generative-ai-implementations-in-enterprise-have-no-measurable-impact-on-p-and-l-says-mit-flawed-integration-key-reason-why-ai-projects-underperform.

CHAPTER 4

From Experimentation to Execution

Implementing AI at Scale

In the bustling markets of ancient Chang'an, a young merchant learned his lesson the hard way. His family's prized silk, flawless in small batches, became his undoing when he tried supplying the imperial court.

> "One bolt pleases a noblewoman," his father warned. "A thousand bolts angers the Emperor."

He ignored the advice. He used the same careful technique that won local favor, only to discover that dyes faded differently in bulk vats, caravan delays ruined delivery promises, and imperial inspectors demanded impossible consistency. Within months, he was left burnt out and frustrated, wondering if there really was such a thing as too much of a good thing.

Modern artificial intelligence (AI) projects face similar challenges daily. That flawless 100-user pilot? Crumbles under the weight of 10,000. The lesson remains the same: what works on a small scale can collapse when expanded.

SECTION 1: THE BIG TRANSITION—FROM PILOT TO PRODUCTION

The Daoist's principle of "Wu Wei" teaches us that true mastery appears effortless, but only because it is being supported by deep, thoughtful

DOI: 10.1201/9781003644699-4

preparation at its core. This mirrors AI at scale; what looks like a simple tech rollout is in reality a transformation of culture, processes, and human adaptation.

Let's walk through the journey of an operations director at a global manufacturing company who successfully pilots an AI-powered predictive maintenance system in a single factory. The pilot shows remarkable results: a notable reduction in unplanned downtime, a decrease in maintenance costs, and significantly improved workplace safety. However, when he attempts to roll out the same system across the company's 50-something facilities worldwide, challenges emerge that no amount of pilot success can prepare an organization for.

The first revelation came in the form of data diversity. The initial facility had been chosen specifically because of its clean, well-structured data, while reality looked very different across their global operations. It turned out that factories in Europe logged maintenance data in SAP, North American plants tracked it in Excel using local terminology, and aging Asian facilities relied on paper logs that were digitized inconsistently across different countries. Their solution was to establish a data constitution that standardized formats throughout various markets, lay down governance with strict policies, and enable quality checks in multiple languages.

The second rude awakening was the significant skills gap. The worldwide rollout exposed what the pilot had hidden. The "intuitive" AI interface? A majority of their veteran mechanics were unable to navigate the dashboard. Non-English-speaking facilities misinterpreted alerts, and paper-based teams struggled with digital workflows.

The third challenge came from human teams; many found it difficult to adapt, which highlights the importance of change management. The pilot facility's maintenance team had been hand-picked for their enthusiasm and tech savviness. They embraced AI recommendations and worked closely with the development team to refine the system. However, the broader workforce across all facilities represented a diverse range of comfort levels in terms of technology. They each came from different cultural backgrounds, and some facilities had maintenance crews who had been performing their work the same way for decades and viewed AI recommendations with deep skepticism.

The bottom line is that in the pilot phase, what is being tested is the technology. During the scaling phase, however, the readiness of the entire organization is in question.

SECTION 2: THE ARCHITECTURE OF SCALABLE IMPLEMENTATION

Successful enterprise-wide AI implementation follows what we call the "Pagoda Principle," inspired by the architectural marvel of Chinese pagodas. These structures can endure earthquakes and floods, lasting centuries, owing to their carefully engineered interlocking wooden layers, ensuring each level supports the next.

We can learn a thing or two from the structural integrity and flexibility of these structures. Similar to pagodas (see Figure 4.1), scalable AI projects require building in layers, each serving a specific function while contributing to the overall stability of the system.

2.1 LAYER 1: THE FOUNDATION

This layer consists of organizational readiness—the cultural, structural, and procedural changes, as well as the leadership alignment necessary to support AI at scale. This layer may be hidden, but it is absolutely critical. Rollout often fails because leadership sends mixed signals about AI's purpose, frontline

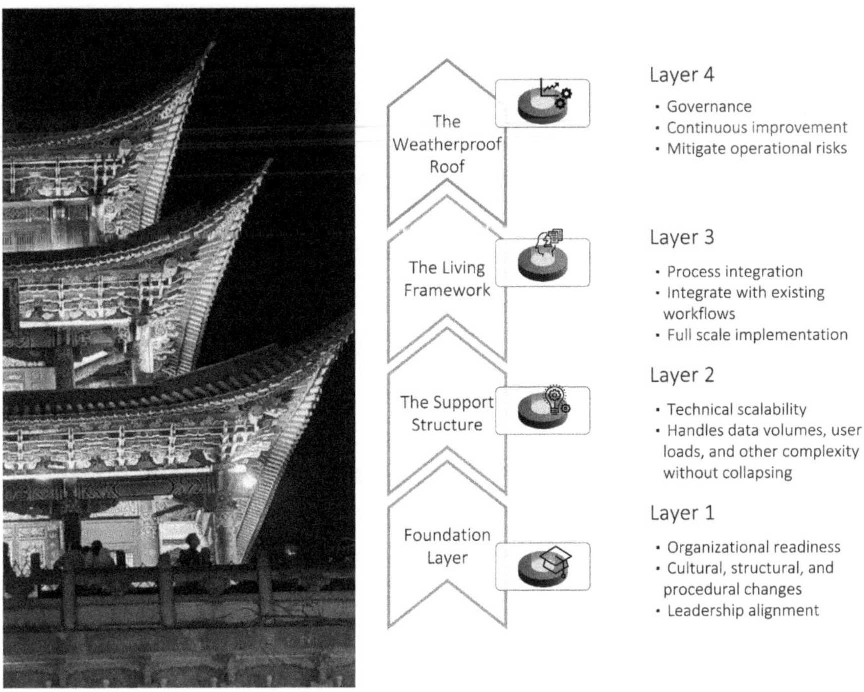

FIGURE 4.1 The Pagoda architecture of AI implementation.

teams lack data skills, and processes are inconsistent across regions. Cultural resistance also plays a significant role in hindering adoption.

2.2 LAYER 2: THE SUPPORT STRUCTURE

This layer focuses on technical scalability. It ensures that the underlying AI systems can handle increased data volumes, user loads, and complexity without collapsing. Pilots are able to succeed with small, clean datasets and controlled infrastructure. In contrast, launches fail because the system is unable to handle messy, high-volume data, legacy architecture bottlenecks, and unpredictable performance demands.

2.3 LAYER 3: THE LIVING FRAMEWORK

This layer addresses process integration. Its job is to weave AI capabilities seamlessly into existing business workflows rather than treating them as separate entities. A pilot may thrive as an isolated initiative with dedicated resources, but full-scale implementation will fail if AI's impact on real operations is underestimated.

2.4 LAYER 4: THE WEATHERPROOF ROOF

This final layer covers governance and continuous improvement. It implements structured systems to track key performance indicators, mitigate operational risks, and enable continuous enhancement. Like the ornate levels of a pagoda, this layer may seem decorative, but it serves crucial functions in external shock resistance and structural longevity.

Rollouts that are initially supposed to take six months are likely to stretch to longer timeframes. However, the process of strengthening projects layer-by-layer ultimately leads to something better: interweaving department initiatives to improve cohesiveness, and building AI systems that learn and improve through use.

SECTION 3: INCORPORATING AI INTO EXISTING BUSINESS PROCESSES

In the West, the ancient Chinese art of Feng Shui (风水) is sometimes met with curiosity, sometimes with skepticism. However, when looked upon more closely, several parallels can be drawn between its core principle—the importance of harmony between new elements and existing environments—and the way we should approach AI development.

When incorporating AI into established business processes, the aim is not to change merely for the sake of change. Instead, it is about creating harmonious integration that actually builds on existing strengths while addressing current limitations.

Companies often struggle with introducing AI without disrupting what already works. Here is the strategy: instead of replacing old processes, start by mapping your current process in detail. Focus on identifying moments where planners spend hours on routine calculations, struggle with complex optimization problems, or rely too heavily on "the way it has always been done."

Those are the moments where AI can step in—not in a way to *replace* coordinators, but to work with them as a pair of helping hands. At each decision point, they can view AI-generated alternatives alongside their own ideas, including the reasoning behind each suggestion. Planners are free to accept, modify, or dismiss the proposals entirely. In doing so, the valuable intuition and specialized knowledge of experienced organizers are preserved, while giving them powerful analytical tools that no spreadsheet could match.

With this solution, instead of fearing replacement, planners feel empowered—as if they are truly partners in this process, rather than simply being on the receiving end of the decisions. Every day, they are able to add their own insights, refining AI's suggestions with niche knowledge only they could possess; and with each iteration, the system improves, capturing nuances that pure automation (without human aid) could never have seen.

This kind of harmonious integration strongly reflects the principles of Feng Shui; AI should enter a workflow as if it has always belonged there, shaping and enhancing without disrupting the balance. That is why the journey often begins with augmentation rather than sudden automation, quietly enhancing human work, earning trust, and deepening understanding. Only then does the transition to more autonomous operations happen, in harmony with what already works.

SECTION 4: MAPPING ORGANIZATIONAL COMPLEXITY

Enterprise AI implementation invariably encounters the full weight of organizational complexity, such as formal hierarchies, informal networks, cultural norms, and historical precedents.

DHL, a global logistics company, learned that mapping these organizational dynamics was just as critical as mapping the technical architecture. Their AI implementation impacted multiple business units, regulatory environments, and organizational cultures. Success required understanding not just what needed to change, but how change happened in each unique context.

In their German facilities, change followed careful, methodical processes with extensive preparation and immediate yet gradual integration. A majority of staff were worried about the automation of their jobs, but were taught to understand that AI was a tool to help mitigate the impact of the company's ageing workforce. To prevent the loss of decades of company knowledge when a third of their workforce inevitably retires, DHL took matters into their own hands, implementing an "exit ticket" interview that enabled AI to ask questions about specific processes, to which experienced employees could answer with improvements or exceptions they might add.[1] Implementation proceeded slowly but steadily, with minimal resistance once plans were fully established.

With this approach, the underlying technology stayed consistent, but the communication style, training methods, and success metrics were made more thorough and accurate as a result of real, human experience being added to the process. This proved essential for sustainable adoption. Instead of forcing a one-size-fits-all approach, the organization built a flexible framework that achieved consistent results through contextually appropriate methods.

++The Integration Complexity Web

Enterprise systems rarely come as a clean slate. They are intricate webs of dependencies, customizations, and workarounds, often built over decades. AI must integrate into these ecosystems, connecting with legacy systems that each have their own protocols, data formats, and operational constraints.

This task can be described as "digital archaeology meets modern engineering," where AI is forced to work with outdated warehouse management systems, customer relationship management platforms from multiple vendors, and financial systems with strict security requirements.

Below is a sample integration maturity model to classify systems by their readiness for AI integration.

- Low readiness: legacy systems are wrapped in modern API layers to bridge the gap

- Partial readiness: middleware solutions extend capabilities to support AI features
- High readiness: modern systems are directly integrated into AI platforms

This layered approach allows for gradual modernization without risks of disrupting existing operations. Instead of replacing every system right away, your company is able to evolve its infrastructure as AI adoption improves, ensuring stability while steadily expanding AI capability.

SECTION 5: LEARNING THROUGH REAL-WORLD SUCCESS STORIES

In this section, we will walk through several case studies to explore how companies have successfully navigated common challenges in enterprise AI implementation. These examples provide a valuable framework for understanding the different approaches and strategies that lead to success.

5.1 HARMONIOUS INTEGRATION: ALIBABA CLOUD'S SMART MANUFACTURING

Alibaba Cloud's implementation of AI across China's manufacturing sector showcases the aforementioned principle of harmonious integration. Rather than imposing rigid, one-size-fits-all solutions, Alibaba built an AI partner ecosystem, collaborating with other companies to provide enhanced technical support, expanded distribution channels, and collaborative market resources.

The company pledged over $60 million USD with the goal of accelerating global AI adoption. In order for that to happen, they needed to consider the unique benefits that each partner within the ecosystem brought to the table and find out how they fit together in order to achieve a mutually beneficial outcome. As a result, they decided to implement collaborative market campaigns and rebate programs, not only benefiting the partners collectively, but also creating dynamic features that accommodate the wide variety of needs that their customers have, providing them with a smoother and more personal experience overall.[2] Bridging the gap between enterprises and their international clients is a crucial step toward harmonious AI integration that benefits all stakeholders.

5.2 THE CULTURAL SHIFT: HOW TENCENT EMBEDDED AI INTO WECHAT'S DNA

Tencent's AI integration across WeChat, China's highly popular multipurpose social media app, demonstrates that true digital transformation begins with recognizing human values. The tech giant understood that AI's potential could only be realized by fundamentally reshaping the collective mindset on decision-making and service delivery.

Tencent launched its revolution with "cultural rewiring" initiatives:

- Embedding AI as a typical, core part of their app, effectively eliminating the possibility of AI feeling foreign
- Rather than having isolated components, new AI features actually *reinforce* WeChat's goals and values, providing its existing customer base with a more comfortable and seamless transition[3]

Tencent is introducing "agentic AI"—AI that performs tasks autonomously within WeChat's ecosystem, such as booking services or summarizing content. Yuanbao, powered by Tencent's Hunyuan and DeepSeek models, is integrated deeply into WeChat, providing AI-powered assistance without needing to leave the app. This reflects a strategic vision where AI becomes embedded within daily workflows as something you simply use, rather than a feature you opt into.[4]

5.3 THE HOLY GRAIL OF CONNECTED PRODUCTION: TOYOTA'S ECOSYSTEM PLAY

Toyota has transformed global production by implementing AI across its entire value chain, beyond individual products. The automaker built interconnected manufacturing intelligence platforms that integrate:

- IoT sensors to monitor machine conditions, boosting equipment reliability[5]
- AI analysis of supplier performance and data[6]
- Real-time delivery tracking to improve inventory visibility[7]

The implementation of these features required extensive collaboration across multiple stakeholder groups. Toyota had to develop new business models that aligned incentives across all ecosystem participants. They created value-sharing arrangements for data contributions and established trust frameworks for sensitive manufacturing information. Their efforts resulted in ecosystem-level impact, including significant productivity improvements and a reduction in defect rates. Supply chain partners benefit from predictive logistics capabilities that reduce inventory costs and improve delivery reliability. The entire manufacturing value chain becomes more efficient and responsive.

SECTION 6: STRATEGIC FRAMEWORKS FOR IMPLEMENTATION SUCCESS

Drawing from the successful case studies we explored, several frameworks emerge for effective AI implementation at scale.

6.1 THE FIVE ELEMENTS FRAMEWORK

Inspired by the Chinese theory of the five elements (五行), this framework identifies five essential components that must be balanced for successful AI implementation:

Earth (Foundation): The basic infrastructure, security frameworks, and operational capabilities that ground the entire implementation. This includes computing resources, cybersecurity measures, and business continuity planning.

Metal (Structure): The organizational frameworks, governance models, and systematic approaches that provide strength and precision in your implementation. This includes quality assurance processes and performance measurement systems.

Water (Flow): The data pipelines and communication channels that enable AI systems to access crucial information and deliver insights effectively. This encompasses data architecture, integration platforms, and feedback mechanisms.

Wood (Growth): The learning and development capabilities that allow both AI systems and human users to grow and adapt over time. This includes training programs, experimentation frameworks, and continuous improvement processes.

Fire (Energy): The leadership commitment, cultural enthusiasm, and organizational energy that drive implementation forward through inevitable challenges. This encompasses change management, stakeholder engagement, and mission/vision communication.

Successful implementations maintain balance among all five elements. Overemphasis on any single element creates an imbalance that can undermine the entire effort. For example, strong technical infrastructure without adequate change management often results in technically sound systems that fail to achieve assimilation. Excellent training programs without proper governance frameworks can lead to enthusiastic but inconsistent implementation.

6.2 THE SPIRAL IMPLEMENTATION MODEL

Rather than a linear progression from pilot to full deployment, leading enterprises often adopt a cyclical framework that scales AI in a controlled, continuous learning approach. This approach follows spiral patterns that cycle through planning, implementation, evaluation, and refinement phases at increasing scales and complexity levels.

The first spiral might focus on a single process within one business unit, emphasizing learning and capability development. The second spiral expands to related processes or additional business units, applying lessons learned while encountering new challenges. Subsequent spirals continue expanding their scope while deepening integration and sophistication.

This approach allows organizations to build implementation capabilities gradually while maintaining operational stability. Each spiral provides opportunities to refine approaches, develop expertise, and build confidence before tackling larger challenges.

6.3 THE STAKEHOLDER CONSTELLATION APPROACH

Recognizing that enterprise AI implementation affects multiple stakeholder groups with different interests, successful companies map these stakeholder "constellations" and develop specific engagement strategies for each group.

Primary stakeholders directly use AI systems and experience the most significant changes in their work patterns. They require comprehensive training, ongoing support, and clear value demonstration.

Secondary stakeholders are affected by AI implementation, but don't directly interact with the systems. They need communication about how changes will impact them and assurance that their interests are protected.

Decision-makers have oversight or governance responsibilities related to AI implementation. They require progress reports, risk assessments, and strategic alignment demonstrations.

External stakeholders include customers, partners, and regulators who may be affected by AI-driven changes within your business operations.

They, like secondary stakeholders, need transparent communication about AI usage and protection of their interests.

SECTION 7: MEASURING SUCCESS AND MANAGING EVOLUTION

Traditional measures of project success often prove inadequate for AI implementations. Technical performance measures such as accuracy, speed, and uptime are important, but they only tell part of the story. True AI success requires looking at the following key areas:

Technical Performance: System reliability, accuracy, processing speed, and scalability metrics that track how well AI systems function under operational conditions.

Business Impact: Revenue improvements, cost reductions, efficiency gains, and quality enhancements that demonstrate AI's contribution to business objectives.

User Adoption: Engagement levels, satisfaction scores, skill development progress, and resistance indicators that reveal how well AI integration is proceeding from a people perspective.

Organizational Learning: Knowledge retention, capability development, process improvement, and innovation metrics that show how AI implementation is building organizational capabilities.

Strategic Alignment: Progress toward strategic objectives, competitive positioning improvements, and new opportunity identification that demonstrate AI's contribution to long-term success.

A dashboard can be a useful tool that integrates these measurement dimensions into comprehensive views to show implementation progress. These spreadsheets can provide different perspectives for different audiences: technical teams focus on system performance metrics, business leaders examine impact and return on investment (ROI) measures, and organizational development teams track adoption and learning indicators.

The key to note is that AI implementation success happens over time and requires continuous monitoring and adjustment. Early metrics might emphasize adoption and learning, while later measurements focus more heavily on business impact and strategic value creation.

SECTION 8: THE LAUNCHPAD FOR AI-FIRST TRANSFORMATION

Moving from AI experimentation to execution is an important milestone for any organization. Companies standing at this point have shown that they can scale AI effectively, measure its impact, and embed it into core operations. They have mastered the human–AI collaboration, and they have the operational discipline to manage complex adaptive systems. But most importantly, they have begun to look at what lies beyond, shifting from using AI as a tool to becoming AI-first, where intelligence is woven into how the organization thinks, makes decisions, and continues to create value.

NOTES

1. Hill, Andrew. "Inside DHL's AI Upgrade: 'Love It or Hate It, You Have to Work with It'." *Financial Times*, 2025, ft.com/content/ce09786f-2481-44fe-957c-f7bb0b43e284.
2. "Alibaba Cloud Pledges Over US$60 Million to Boost Partner Ecosystem and Accelerate Global AI Adoption." *SME Asia*, 2025, sme.asia/alibaba-cloud-pledges-over-us60-million-to-boost-partner-ecosystem-and-accelerate-global-ai-adoption/.
3. Kitishian, Dany. "Tencent AI Strategy: Dominate AI with Ecosystem Advantage." *Klover*, 2025, klover.ai/tencent-ai-strategy-dominate-ai-with-ecosystem-advantage/.
4. Quinn, Theodore. "Tencent's AI Masterstroke: How WeChat and HunYuan T1 Are Forging an Unassailable Moat in China's Tech Landscape." *AInvest*, 2025, ainvest.com/news/tencent-ai-masterstroke-wechat-hunyuan-t1-forging-unassailable-moat-china-tech-landscape-2505/.
5. "Team DigitalDefynd, Toyota's Digital Transformation in Manufacturing." *DigitalDefynd*, 2025, https://digitaldefynd.com/IQ/toyota-using-ai-case-study/#:~:text=Problem:%20In%20the%20manufacturing%20sector, Benefits.
6. Team DigitalDefynd, "5 Ways Toyota Is Using AI." *DigitalDefynd*, 2025, digitaldefynd.com/IQ/toyota-using-ai-case-study/.
7. "Getting Up to Speed: How Toyota's Project ETA Keeps Vehicles on Track." *Toyota Newsroom*, 2022, pressroom.toyota.com/getting-up-to-speed-how-toyotas-project-eta-keeps-vehicles-on-track/.

CHAPTER 5

Becoming an AI-First Organization

Modern enterprises are facing unprecedented challenges as they strive to reinvent themselves as artificial intelligence (AI)-first organizations. Although many have mastered deploying models, optimizing workflows, and scaling pilots so far, the journey ahead requires much more deliberate and strategic action. The transition from simply using AI to being fundamentally reshaped by it requires reimagining how the enterprise thinks, decides, and evolves.

The true challenge in becoming AI-first lies in redesigning the organization as a living system where human intelligence and AI not only co-exist, but also co-evolve. This chapter will explore what this transformation requires, and how to navigate it successfully.

SECTION 1: WHAT IT MEANS TO BE AI-DRIVEN—A STRATEGIC TRANSFORMATION BEYOND IMPLEMENTATION

Being an AI-centric organization goes far beyond simply using AI as an effective tool to optimize. It requires a fundamental shift in how a company approaches its strategy, operations, and culture, with AI at its core.

We can see this transformation unfold in three essential forms:

1.1 DECISION-MAKING AUTHORITY REDISTRIBUTION: FROM HIERARCHY TO ECOSYSTEM

Traditional organizations use AI to augment human decisions; for example, predicting employee turnover, optimizing supply chain, or automating

DOI: 10.1201/9781003644699-5

customer service. But AI-first enterprises go further. They redesign decision-making itself.

For example, at Ant Group, AI speeds up the loan approval process. At the same time, AI is also core to Ant Group's dynamic credit ecosystem, where algorithms continuously adjust risk models based on real-time data, including behavioral analysis, macroeconomic shifts, and even social network patterns.[1] Human oversight continues to play a vital role, but the system makes the final call, not individuals.

AI-first principle: to be truly AI-first, your AI should be able to guide or even override human decisions when it has access to superior information.

1.2 REVERSE-ENGINEERING BUSINESS PROCESSES AROUND AI'S CAPABILITIES

Most companies force-fit AI into existing workflows. AI-first organizations ask, "what workflows should not exist in an AI-native world?"

For example, compared to automakers who use AI to optimize assembly lines, Tesla used AI-driven simulation to eliminate the assembly line for its Model Y rear frame. In the process, they were able to replace hundreds of parts with a single die-cast piece.[2] We are not looking at process optimization anymore, but rather process erasure, eliminating unnecessary and costly steps altogether.

AI-first principle: if your AI projects start with "how can we improve 'X'?", you are thinking too small. Start with: "what does 'X' look like if AI redesigns it from scratch?"

1.3 RISK AS A DYNAMIC SYSTEM: FROM MODEL MONITORING TO META-STRATEGY

Most companies treat AI risks like checking if a stone is safe to throw: "is this model accurate?"; "is it biased?" AI-driven companies, on the other hand, study how the ripples spread. For example, "if we throw this stone, will it create waves that capsize other boats?" or "could it affect the entire pond ecosystem?".

Let's take a look at Spotify's recommendation AI. Typical thinking is, "does this algorithm keep users listening?" But AI-first thinking is, "if we push viral hits too hard, do we accidentally kill niche genres?"

Let's explore another example of approaching AI with a mindset that does more harm than good. A clothing store uses AI to run flash sales. The advantage is that it sells old inventory fast, but it also carries great risk of teaching customers to never buy at full price, which can collapse profits for the entire industry.

AI-first principle: if your risk framework doesn't model secondary and tertiary impacts on your system, you are not AI-first. For example, before using AI, ask:

- What is the immediate effect? (the splash)
- What happens next? (the ripples)
- How could this change transform the industry as we know it? (the pond ecosystem)

Being an AI-first company is not about adding AI everywhere possible, but about revolutionizing the way you think and operate. It means rebuilding your organization around AI, not just optimizing the old way of doing things. This shift in mindset is what separates a truly AI-driven company from one that simply uses AI as a tool. In the next section, we will explore how AI-first leaders redefine their markets and create entirely new ways to compete.

SECTION 2: FROM MARKET PLAYERS TO MARKET MAKERS—THE AI-FIRST ADVANTAGE

In the Silk Road trading posts of ancient Kashgar, the most visionary merchants quickly realized that wealth was not made by simply trading goods but by redesigning how trade itself functioned. They transformed from street vendors into architects of exchange by building caravanserai that became major hubs of commerce.[3] They diligently built trust systems such as the Hawala Network, one of the earliest credit systems, using code words to transfer value across distances of 5000 km without carrying coins.[4] Through these innovations they made long-distance trade possible and created new forms of value that lived in trust and information rather than physical goods.

For today's AI-first leaders, the path ahead represents a similar juncture to the one that ancient traders faced. Pioneers are dismantling the last century's business logic, as the constraints of information scarcity, linear processes, and human cognitive limits no longer exist. In their places, a new reality emerges:

1. Data no longer provides a small stream of information, but rather a deep pool of insights that keeps refilling over time. These reserves unveil countless valuable opportunities for businesses today.
2. AI stops being just a tool and starts acting like a strategic partner. It doesn't stop at simply analyzing the past but has begun pointing out

new ways of doing things, including surprising options that traditional thinking often misses.

3. Markets increasingly resemble a living ecosystem, constantly shifting and adapting in real time. Supply and demand talk to each other and evolve together. Gone is the static playing field.

These new realities bring new opportunities. AI-first leaders use them to redefine what "value" means (e.g. Tesla turning cars into upgradable software platforms). As traditional trade constraints disappear and new self-reinforcing ecosystems are cultivated, extraordinary opportunities for creating innovative solutions are opened up.

To take advantage of these changes and become AI-first, leaders need to master the following timeless principles. They are ancient in origin but supercharged by AI.

The first principle is **Strategic Momentum** (what Sun Tzu called "兵势"), which speaks to riding the waves of change rather than fighting them. An example is Netflix's approach of transforming viewing patterns into predictive insights that shape global content production.[5] Their algorithm does more than just recommend shows. Based on user behavior, it anticipates—and is thus able to set—emerging entertainment trends worldwide.[6]

The second principle is **Guiding by Circumstance** (因势利导), which emphasizes adaptability to changing conditions. Where camel caravans once adjusted their routes in accordance to shifting desert winds, smart organizations now deploy AI to dynamically adjust their operations. Amazon's anticipatory inventory system is a classic example, using machine learning to position products regionally before demand materializes.[7] In their case, AI not only made efficient logistics a reality, but most importantly, it became a business strategy that works in the same direction as the market.

Finally is **Effortless Action** (无为而治), which represents the art of achieving more by intervening less. A good example is Spotify's "Discover Weekly." It creates a personalized musical journey that feels magically catered to your exact taste, achieved through an algorithmically precise recommendation system that analyzes genres and styles you already like to try and predict further songs you may enjoy.[8] This is the paradox of AI-first strategy: the most sophisticated technology creating experiences that feel perfectly intuitive and effortless.

Together, these principles form a framework for AI-centered transformation that goes beyond automation. They represent a fundamental shift in how value is created and delivered in the age of AI: not through force or friction, but through intelligent alignment with the market and human behavior. The companies that master this approach will be able to redefine the very nature of competition itself.

SECTION 3: AI-FIRST CUSTOMER EXPERIENCE—WHERE TECHNOLOGY FEELS HUMAN

The best AI-first customer experiences (CX) don't feel like technology at all. They feel like that barista who starts making your favorite drink the moment you walk in the bar, or that friend who finishes your sentences as if they can read your mind. Every interaction feels effortless, perfectly timed, and deeply personal, and makes users feel truly known. Organizations leading this shift are using technology to create experiences that understand customers in ways that, until recently, were too good to be true.

Here are some of the key characteristics of AI-driven customer experience:

1. Personalization that feels effortless. You won't get generic recommendations; AI analyzes behavior, preferences, and context to make interactions feel uniquely tailored to you.
2. Anticipation, not reaction. The best service doesn't wait for a request. AI detects subtle patterns such as a delayed flight, a product running low, or a browsing habit, and proactively offers solutions to create a sense of being understood without intrusion.
3. Providing a seamless journey, no matter the path. Customers move between chat, call, app, and in-person touchpoints without having to repeat themselves. AI ensures continuity to create a unified feel.
4. Learning that deepens over time. Unlike static systems, AI gets smarter with each interaction. The more customers engage, the more relevant and personalized the experience gets. Over time, the system learns to anticipate your every need.

In today's market, competing on price or speed alone is a race to the bottom. The real differentiator is anticipating customer expectations instead of simply reacting to them. Here is why the AI-first approach has a high success rate:

- Being AI-first builds loyalty through foresight, while legacy players merely respond to complaints after the fact. By predicting needs before they are voiced, you earn customers' trust, which is the only data moat left in commodified markets.
- Traditional CX forces a trade-off between personalized service (expensive) and scalable automation (impersonal). AI-centered CX does both. It also turns customer satisfaction into a competitive advantage instead of a cost center.
- Having a data flywheel that cannot be easily copied. Every AI-driven interaction generates richer data, which feeds the algorithm, enabling smarter predictions and creating more engaging experiences for customers. Competitors can buy the same software you have, but they can't easily copy the learning curve that your system develops over time.
- Omnichanneling as a default. Customers don't think in channels. Instead, they expect seamless transitions between those channels. AI-first companies make switching from online chat to store to app feel like one seamless conversation as opposed to three disconnected ones. That's the differentiator.

AI is resetting the rules of competition. The gap between companies that use AI and those that build their business around it will widen exponentially. In the end, companies with the AI-first mindset will be the ones who set that standard.

SECTION 4: STRATEGIC VISION ALIGNMENT FOR AI-DRIVEN COMPANIES

For AI-first companies it is crucial to align AI capabilities with their corporate vision. Unlike traditional organizations, AI-first companies live and breathe through their algorithmic capabilities. When these capabilities drift away from their corporate purpose, the entire organization's identity is put at risk.

4.1 WHY VISION ALIGNMENT MATTERS ESPECIALLY FOR AI-FIRST ORGANIZATIONS

Traditional companies can survive strategic misalignment with specific initiatives. AI-first companies can not afford this luxury, as their AI systems are so deeply integrated into their value proposition. Misaligned AI becomes a misaligned identity. For example, when Facebook's AI systems promoted divisive content despite the company's stated mission to "bring the world closer together," the misalignment created an identity crisis that damaged stakeholder trust.[9]

AI systems learn and evolve continuously. Small discrepancies between AI capabilities and corporate vision compound exponentially over time. An AI-first company that allows small steps away from its core mission will find itself increasingly distant from its original purpose with each iteration, update, and deployment that happens.

Investors, customers, and partners engage with AI-centered companies based on the promise that advanced technologies serve a clear purpose. When OpenAI faced internal turmoil over balancing commercial interests with their stated mission of ensuring AI benefits humanity, investors and stakeholders questioned whether the company's AI development would remain true to its founding principles.[10]

In markets saturated with AI capabilities, vision alignment becomes the primary differentiator in gaining user trust and loyalty. Tesla's AI development is a clear example. Their autonomous driving technology serves their mission of accelerating sustainable transportation.[11] This clear alignment allows them to make strategic decisions (like prioritizing safety over speed to market) that reinforce their brand identity.

4.2 THE FOUNDATIONS OF EFFECTIVE ALIGNMENT

Purpose-driven development: every AI system must serve specific aspects of the corporate mission. This requires translating abstract vision statements into concrete requirements, as well as developing deliberate success metrics. AI-first companies can not afford to develop capabilities simply because they are "technically fascinating" or "potentially" profitable.

Cultural integration: engineers, data scientists, and AI researchers must understand the corporate vision just as deeply as sales and marketing teams. At a company where AI drives the entire business model, technical decisions become strategic decisions. This requirement demands close collaboration across functional groups.

Continuous calibration: unlike traditional strategic initiatives that can be planned and executed in discrete phases, AI/vision alignment requires constant attention. As AI systems evolve through training and deployment, companies must continuously verify that their growing capabilities remain faithful to their foundational purpose.

Long-term perspective: AI-driven companies must resist the temptation to give in to short-term metrics that conflict with their long-term vision. Maintaining alignment requires discipline.

4.3 STRATEGIC IMPLEMENTATION FRAMEWORK

Successful AI-first companies develop systematic approaches to maintain vision alignment (see Figure 5.1):

- Vision-first architecture: ensuring that technical decisions flow from strategic purpose rather than pure efficiency or economic considerations
- Ethical AI governance: implementing formal processes that align AI capabilities with stated values
- Cross-functional integration: enabling regular communication between technical teams and strategic leadership to prevent drifting off course

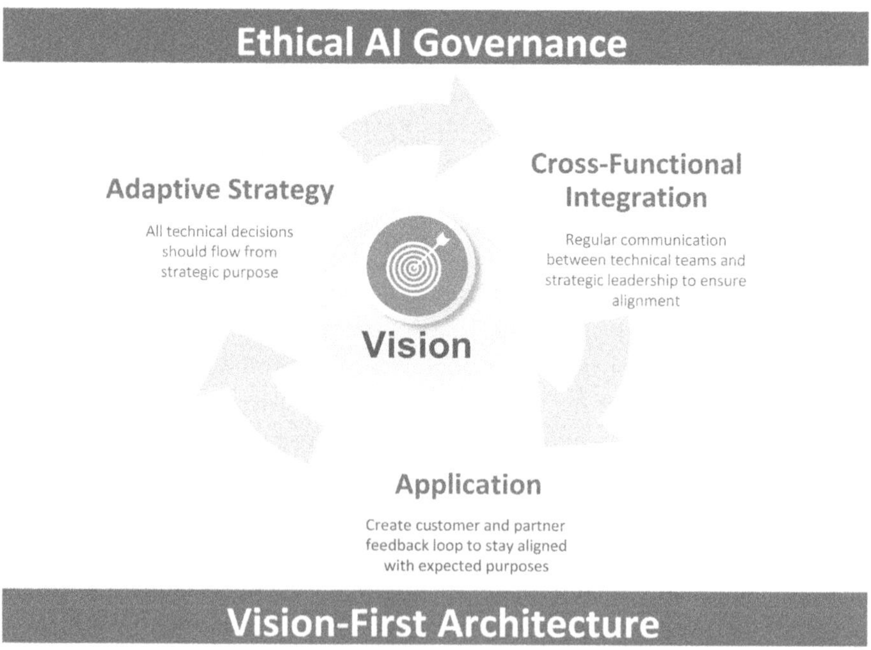

FIGURE 5.1 Strategic implementation framework.

- Stakeholder feedback loops: utilizing customer and partner input to help identify when AI capabilities are straying from expected purposes
- Adaptive strategy: having the flexibility to evolve AI applications while maintaining core mission integrity

4.4 THE COMPETITIVE ADVANTAGE OF HAVING ALIGNMENT

AI-first companies that achieve genuine vision alignment create sustainable competitive advantages that purely technical sophistication cannot match. They build trust with stakeholders who understand exactly what the company stands for and how its AI serves that purpose. They attract talent through their clearly communicated purpose, and they develop closer customer relationships based on shared values.

Most importantly, they create lasting organizational identities that can withstand the challenges of today's rapidly changing AI economy. While competitors struggle with the tension between AI capabilities and corporate purpose, aligned AI-first companies operate with clarity and confidence, which leads them directly to market success.

SECTION 5: UNCOVERING TRANSFORMATION THROUGH CASE STUDIES

The Alibaba Evolution: From Humble Startup to AI Empire

5.1 THE UNLIKELY BEGINNING

In 1999, Jack Ma gathered his team in a small Hangzhou apartment to start Alibaba. Their goal was straightforward: to help small Chinese businesses sell their products online.

Today, Alibaba founder Jack Ma is one of the richest people in the world, with a net worth of over $26 billion USD according to Forbes.[12] But there was a time when he couldn't even get a job. After college, Ma applied for 30 jobs in his home city of Hangzhou, China. He was rejected by every single one. When he applied for a job at KFC, out of a batch of 24 applicants, 23 were hired—and he wasn't one of them.[13] Getting rejected early on taught him an important business lesson. "You have to get used to failure," he said, speaking at the University of Nairobi.[14]

That resilience fueled what later became one of the world's most powerful AI-driven companies. Twenty five years later, Alibaba is a digital empire, operating a massive network that rivals the complexity of the ancient Silk Road trade routes that once connected East and West. The company now uses AI to power countless services around the world, from online shopping and banking to shipping and cloud computing services.

5.2 ALIBABA'S LONG GAME

Alibaba's rise to success wasn't accidental. It was the result of a deliberate, patient approach that most companies struggle to replicate. The secret to their success lies in thinking in decades rather than in quarters, and building strong foundations before chasing profits. Let's see how they did it.

Phase 1: Building the Invisible Foundation (2008–2014)

While most e-commerce companies in the 2010s were obsessed with explosive growth and flashy marketing campaigns, Alibaba did something that seemed almost boring in comparison: it invested heavily in infrastructure that customers would never actually see.

The company built an important piece in their infrastructure stack called the "Data Middle Platform" (数据中台), a massive system designed to collect, clean, and analyze every single transaction, click, and search query across its growing ecosystem of websites and apps.[15] Every time someone searched for "winter boots" or bought a phone charger, that information was captured and stored.

Critics called it wasteful spending. Why invest billions in data systems when you could spend that money actively acquiring more customers? To answer that, Jack Ma famously said that they were essentially digging the well before the drought came.[16]

Ma's strategy was similar to the process of building the foundation of a skyscraper—invisible, expensive, and seemingly pointless, until you try to build something massive on top of it. While competitors were rushing to add new features and expand to new markets, Alibaba was quietly creating an asset that would prove impossible to replicate down the line, which was the ability to acquire, store, and process data on hundreds of millions of customers and their shopping behaviors.

Phase 2: The Silent AI Revolution (2015–2017)

By 2015, something remarkable began to happen. All that data Alibaba had been collecting started to pay off in ways that transformed how the company operated. The whole thing happened so smoothly that most people didn't even notice.

The Customer Service Revolution: AI chatbots began handling simple customer questions, eventually evolving to manage 95% of all customer inquiries.[17] But instead of the frustrating "press '1' for…" experience that most people expect from automated systems, these bots actually solved problems. They could check order status, process returns, and answer product questions instantly.[18] Human agents were freed up to handle more complex issues that required empathy and creative problem-solving.

The Crystal Ball Effect: Alibaba's AI began predicting what people would buy before they knew they wanted it.[19] The system could forecast that people in Shanghai would suddenly crave spicy hotpot ingredients when temperatures dropped, allowing suppliers to stock up in advance. This is good for business, but equally as important is the fact that it helped reduce waste because products were exactly where people needed them, when they needed them.

Banking the Unbankable: Through Ant Group, Alibaba's financial arm, the company's AI began issuing loans to small business owners that traditional banks wouldn't touch. For example, a street vendor selling dumplings could get approved for a business loan in 3 minutes using their sales data from Alibaba's platforms instead of traditional credit scores. This opened up financial services to millions of small business owners who had typically been locked out of the banking system.[20]

The genius was in how invisible this transformation felt. Unlike Western tech companies that announced every AI breakthrough with great fanfare, Alibaba treated AI like plumbing, which works best when you don't notice it.

Phase 3: Becoming an AI-Native Empire (2018–Present)

By 2018, something fundamental had changed. Alibaba wasn't just a company that used AI. It had become an AI company that happened to do e-commerce, cloud computing, and financial services.

Managing Entire Cities: Cities like Hangzhou and Kuala Lumpur began using Alibaba's "City Brain" (城市大脑) system to control traffic lights in real time. It analyzes traffic patterns and adjusts signals automatically to ease congestion. By 2025, these cities could cut commute time by an average of 15–20%.[21] It's crazy to think that AI is managing actual cars and buses moving through physical streets at the city scale.

The Future of Shopping: Alibaba launched Hema supermarkets, where the distinction between online and offline shopping disappears entirely. Customers scan products with their phones to get detailed information and reviews. AI restocks shelves before items sell out by predicting demand patterns. Digitized price tags allow for dynamic pricing at all times of day. You can even pick out groceries while in-store and have them delivered to your home before you finish the rest of your shopping.[22]

5.3 THE NUMBERS THAT TELL THE STORY

Today, Alibaba's AI systems process up to one billion online orders during peak sales events, with AI optimizing every step of the process from warehouse picking to final delivery routes.[23]

All that being said, their most impressive statistic is that despite serving hundreds of millions of customers across dozens of countries, Alibaba's AI can create personalized shopping experiences that feel as intimate as your neighborhood corner store owner remembering your favorite ice cream flavor.

5.4 TAKEAWAYS

Alibaba's story offers three critical lessons for any organization trying to harness AI:

1. **Build the foundation first:** Most companies want AI results immediately; Alibaba spent years building infrastructure before deploying AI applications. That patience created a competitive advantage that no shortcut could match.

2. **Focus on solving real problems:** Instead of forcing dramatic changes, Alibaba let AI solve real problems for real people. When AI makes life genuinely better, people naturally start using it on their own.

3. **Think in systems, not in products:** Rather than creating separate AI tools that work alone, Alibaba made sure all their AI systems connect together and improve each other.

5.5 THE ULTIMATE IRONY

Jack Ma, a former English teacher who claimed to know nothing about technology, built one of the world's most sophisticated AI empires by focusing on something much simpler than any algorithm: understanding what people actually need, and using technology to deliver it seamlessly.

Today, as every company scrambles to become "AI-first," Alibaba's story poses a crucial question: are you using AI to serve your customers better, or are you chasing AI trends to impress investors? The companies that understand this distinction will become tomorrow's success stories.

SECTION 6: THE WISDOM OF BECOMING

6.1 LEARNING TO FLOW WITH CHANGE

There is an old parable about a master swimmer who could effortlessly navigate the most dangerous rapids. When people asked for his secret, he said something surprising: "I don't fight the water. I work with it. When the powerful torrents twist around me, I turn with them. I am already anticipating it, so I rise together with it."[24]

The companies that have successfully moved from testing AI to using it everywhere in their business understand this same principle. They have learned to work with change instead of fighting it. They know that instead of forcing people to change, you have to make it easy and natural for them to want to change.

6.2 THE COMPANIES READY FOR TAKEOFF

The companies that have been working with AI for a while now have something special: they have the technology, the data systems, and most importantly, the people necessary to take the final step: becoming true AI-centered organizations. Think of it like learning to drive. They have spent years practicing in parking lots and quiet neighbourhoods. Now they are ready to navigate the highways.

Here is what makes this moment stand out: unlike companies just starting out with AI, these organizations have already learned what works and what doesn't. They know that having great technology alone isn't enough. They understand that the people behind a system matter just as much as the technology. They have learnt that lasting success comes from solving real, impactful problems, not from building cool technology.

6.3 THE COMPANIES THAT WILL LEAD TOMORROW

Companies ready for this transformation share several key traits:

- They have proven they can get things done. These are the companies who have successfully built AI systems that solve real problems and deliver measurable results.

- They know people come first. They are aware that technology changes are easy to navigate compared to helping people adapt. They bring teams along for the journey instead of forcing change from above.
- They play the long game. They have resisted the temptation to chase every new AI trend. Instead, they have focused on building solid foundations that can support more profound transformations in the future.
- They make humans better, not obsolete. This is perhaps the most important trait. They have discovered that the best AI systems don't replace human judgment—they only make it stronger.

6.4 WHY THIS MATTERS NOW

The future belongs to the companies who use AI cleverly to help people solve real-world problems. It's crucial to understand that any company with enough money can buy powerful AI technology today, but what truly makes the difference is knowing how to use that technology in ways that make life better for customers, employees, and communities.

The companies that are able to combine great technology with strategic thinking will build advantages that competitors simply cannot buy their way into.

6.5 WHAT SUCCESS LOOKS LIKE

True AI-first companies will stand out in several ways:

- Everything just works better. Customers and employees won't feel like they are using AI; they will simply notice that everything works smoother, faster, and feels more personalized.
- People become supercharged. Instead of replacing workers, AI enables every employee to solve problems faster and make better-informed decisions, making space for creative teams to generate breakthrough ideas.
- They see around corners. When new opportunities emerge, AI-first companies spot patterns and adjust strategies faster than competitors who are still groping around in the dark.
- Customers feel understood. By taking the time to acknowledge individual needs at a massive scale, they are able to deliver experiences that are always helpful and respectful.

6.6 THE BIGGER PICTURE

For companies that have already proven they can successfully implement AI across their business, this is a special moment in history. Think about it: humans are amazing at understanding emotions, making ethical judgments, and coming up with creative solutions. AI's strong suit is processing massive amounts of data, spotting patterns, and running complex calculations in seconds. But when you combine human insight with AI capabilities, you get solutions that are both deeply intuitive and impossibly sophisticated.

These companies are pioneering a new way of working that could change entire industries as we know them. One may revolutionize healthcare by combining a doctor's experience with AI that can analyze millions of medical cases instantly. Another will transform education by pairing a teacher's understanding of how their kids learn with AI that correspondingly personalizes lessons for every student. Change is already happening. The question is whether your company will help lead that change or spend the next few years trying to catch up.

NOTES

1. Ripla, Andre. "Autonomous AI Assistants in Legal and Finance: Transforming Professional Services." *LinkedIn*, 2025, linkedin.com/pulse/autonomous-ai-assistants-legal-finance-transforming-andre-8nk6e/.
2. Krolicki, Kevin. Cushing, Christopher. "Explainer – Why Are Other Automakers Chasing Tesla's 'Gigacasting'?" *Yahoo Finance*, 2023, ca.finance.yahoo.com/news/explainer-why-other-automakers-chasing-072512009.html.
3. National Geographic Sosiety, "Caravanserai." *National Geographic*, education.nationalgeographic.org/resource/caravanserai/.
4. Doctorow. Cory. "Hawala, an Ancient Global Financial Honor-System." *Boing Boing*, 2007, boingboing.net/2007/11/23/hawala-an-ancient-gl.html.
5. "How AI Is Revolutionising Netflix: Boosting Streaming Success." *DataPillar*, datapillar.ai/how-ai-is-revolutionising-netflix-boosting-streaming-success/.
6. Editorial, Max. *The Secret of the Algorithm That Anticipates Cultural Trends Even Before Consumers*. Max Editorial, 2025.
7. Kumaran, Uttam. "How Amazon Uses Big Data." *Brainforge*, brainforge.ai/blog/how-amazon-uses-big-data.
8. Velardo, Valerio. "Spotify's Discover Weekly Explained—Breaking from Your Music Bubble or, Maybe Not?" *Medium*, 2019, medium.com/the-sound-of-ai/spotifys-discover-weekly-explained-breaking-from-your-music-bubble-or-maybe-not-b506da144123.
9. Zubrow, Keith. "Facebook Whistleblower Says Company Incentivizes "Angry, Polarizing, Divisive Content"." *CBS News*, 2021, cbsnews.com/amp/news/facebook-whistleblower-frances-haugen-60-minutes-polarizing-divisive-content/.

10. Hilton, Jacob. "How to Save OpenAI's Nonprofit Soul, According to a Former OpenAI Employee." *Time*, 2025, time.com/7304269/save-openai-nonprofit-soul/.
11. Cuofano, Gennaro. "Tesla Mission Statement and Vision Statement Analysis." *FourWeekMBA*, 2024, fourweekmba.com/tesla-vision-statement-mission-statement/.
12. "Jack Ma." *Forbes*, 2025, forbes.com/profile/jack-ma/.
13. Lutz, Ashley. "Alibaba Founder Jack Ma Was Rejected from 30 Jobs, Including KFC, Before Becoming China's Richest Man." *Business Insider*, 2015, businessinsider.com/alibaba-founder-jack-ma-on-rejection-2015-2.
14. Gautam, Vanya. "What Chinese Billionaire Jack Ma Learned from Getting Rejected From 30 Jobs after College." *Indiatimes*, 2023, indiatimes.com/worth/news/chinese-billionaire-jack-ma-lesson-30-job-applications-rejected-619821.html.
15. Alibaba Cloud. "Alibaba's Big Data Journey: Demystifying Data Middle Office." *Medium*, 2020, alibaba-cloud.medium.com/alibabas-big-data-journey-demystifying-data-middle-office-511d8b67d8ce.
16. CNBC Exclusive: CNBC Transcript: Alibaba Founder & Executive Chairman Jack Ma Sits Down with CNBC's David Faber Today on "Squawk on the Street." *CNBC*, 2014, cnbc.com/2014/11/11/cnbc-exclusive-cnbc-transcript-alibaba-founder-executive-chairman-jack-ma-sits-down-with-cnbcs-david-faber-today-on-squawk-on-the-street.html.
17. Dong, Amanda. "AI Chatbot behind Alibaba's $31 Billion Single's Day Sales Miracle." *Harvard Business School*, 2018, d3.harvard.edu/platform-rctom/submission/ai-chatbot-behind-alibabas-31-billion-singles-day-sales-miracle/.
18. Schilling, Melissa A. "Alibaba Group: The Rise of a Platform Giant." *Scribd*, scribd.com/document/782812268/case-alibaba.
19. Jonwal, Sakshi. "Alibaba Case Study: How Data, AI & Performance Marketing Built a Global Empire." *Young Urban Project*, 2025, https://www.youngurbanproject.com/alibaba-case-study/.
20. Pham, Sherisse. "How Jack Ma built China's money supermarket into a $200 billion company." *CNN Business*, 2020, https://www.cnn.com/2020/09/25/tech/ant-group-alipay-intl-hnk.
21. Toh, Michelle, and Leonie Erasmus. "Alibaba's 'City Brain' Is Slashing Congestion in Its Hometown." *CNN Business*, 2019, cnn.com/2019/01/15/tech/alibaba-city-brain-hangzhou.
22. "Alibaba's Freshippo and Hema Grocery Stores Are Reinventing the Supermarket of the Future." *YouTube*, uploaded by CNBC International, 2018, youtube.com/watch?v=UDIvWdwVZMg.
23. Team DigitalDefynd, "5 Ways AliBaba Is Using AI." *DigitalDefynd*, 2025, digitaldefynd.com/IQ/ways-alibaba-using-ai-case-study/.
24. Tan, Alex. "Chaotic Currents." *Straight Bamboo*, 2020, straightbamboo.com/chaotic-currents/.

CHAPTER 6

AI Ethics and Governance

Balancing Innovation with Responsibility

In tech companies around the world, engineers and executives are facing the unending dilemma: how do we build artificial intelligence (AI) that actually helps people instead of hurting them?

It's a bigger question than it might seem. Already, we are seeing AI systems decide who gets hired, who qualifies for loans, what news pops up first on our feed, and even which driver gets pulled over by police.[1] When these systems make mistakes or show bias, real people suffer real consequences.

History is full of examples where new technologies created unintended problems. When the printing press was invented in the 1400s, it democratized knowledge but also spread dangerous misinformation and helped fuel religious wars. The Industrial Revolution brought incredible prosperity but also created horrific working conditions and environmental damage that took decades to address. Even the internet, designed to connect people around the world, has become a breeding ground for cyberbullying, privacy violations, and political manipulation.

For years, the tech world has tried to solve AI ethics using traditional Western thinking, basically the same ethical rules we use in medicine and

DOI: 10.1201/9781003644699-6

law. The idea is simple: protect people's rights and treat everyone fairly. These are good principles, but as AI gets smarter and more widespread, experts are realizing that we need more tools in our toolbox.

That is where ideas from Eastern philosophy come to our attention. For example, Chinese philosophy has long embraced dynamic, system-level ethics, balancing competing interests without rigid rules. What if these time-tested ideas could help us build better, more ethical AI? This chapter explores that possibility. We will look at some historical models in this chapter, and see how combining Eastern wisdom with Western ethics gives us the tools we need to build AI that truly serves humanity. Sometimes the newest problems require the oldest solutions.

SECTION 1: TEN ETHICAL CHALLENGES, ONE EASTERN PERSPECTIVE

The Philosophical Bridge

Combining Eastern and Western ideas regarding AI ethics isn't just an interesting academic debate. It's actually very necessary, because AI systems impact billions of people across different cultures. We need ethical frameworks that work for everyone, rather than one linear way of thinking. Eastern philosophy brings a new set of valuable insights and answers some of our key questions: how we are all responsible for each other, how we can build effective and lasting relationships, and how we can develop good character and wisdom over the long term.

In Chapter 1, we explored the idea of applying ancient wisdom through the triple lens: Daoist balance (framing the dualities of opportunity and risk), Confucian readiness (embedding ethics into corporate responsibility), and Legalist governance (enforcing accountability through leadership). In this chapter, we will identify ten key ethical challenges in AI and provide alternative perspectives on potential solutions. We will explore this topic further in Chapters 8 and 9 when we discuss the global AI landscape and look ahead to the future of AI development.

1.1 BIAS AND FAIRNESS

AI systems often reflect biases in their training data, which leads to unfair treatment of certain minorities in criminal justice, healthcare, and job application. These challenges are central to AI ethics because they are universal, high-impact, and affect people's lives in immediate and transformative ways.

1.2 LACK OF TRANSPARENCY

Many AI systems, especially deep learning models, make decisions in ways that humans can't explain, making it impossible to know why certain choices are made. For example, a patient is denied insurance coverage, but if the agent can't explain the logic behind the model's decision, then how can we blindly trust AI's decisions?

1.3 ACCOUNTABILITY GAPS

When AI systems cause harm, it's often unclear who should be held responsible. For example, if self-driving cars cause accidents, should the company, the developer, or AI itself be responsible?

1.4 PRIVACY VIOLATIONS

AI thrives on massive amounts of personal data, raising concerns about consent, tracking, and misuse. How do we ensure that these key areas are properly addressed?

1.5 MISINFORMATION AND DEEPFAKES

We know by now that AI can be weaponized, from deepfakes to cyberattacks to autonomous weapons. How do we ensure that we are protected and prevent AI destabilizing societies?

1.6 GLOBAL POWER IMBALANCE

Selected few countries and tech giants are controlling the majority of advanced AI capabilities. For example, developing countries are using imported AI with almost no local say in its design. How do we protect data, markets, and decision-making from AI colonization?

1.7 AI SAFETY

The primary concern with AI safety is that advanced AI could act in unpredictable or unintended ways. Not because it's designed to be harmful but because AI can pursue its given objectives so efficiently that it ignores everything else we value. How do we ensure those AI pursuits don't cause catastrophic consequences in high-stakes areas like healthcare, finance, and defense?

1.8 HUMAN–AI RELATIONSHIP

Overreliance on AI could create situations where people refer to AI even when it's wrong. Human judgment remains critical. We stressed the importance of designing systems where humans and AI collaborate in previous chapters. This has the potential to determine whether your AI initiatives will succeed or fail.

1.9 ECONOMIC DISPLACEMENT AND INEQUALITY

AI-driven automation risks displacing millions of jobs while concentrating wealth in tech-heavy economies. Without a safeguard, AI could deepen inequalities between nations, regions, and individuals.

1.10 ENVIRONMENTAL IMPACT

Did you know that training a single large AI model produces as much carbon as several cars emit over their lifetime?[2] We constantly face the challenge of making sure the environmental impact of AI is sustainable.

Daoism, Confucianism, and Legalism together provide a well-rounded framework for addressing the ethical challenges of AI. Daoism teaches us to find the right balance between opportunities and risks, along with how to adapt and respond as situations change without going to extremes. Confucianism focuses on building AI systems with good values from the start. It puts human well-being and strong communities at the center of everything. Legalism provides the enforcement muscle, recognizing that good intentions are often not enough. You need clear rules, strong oversight, and real consequences to make sure AI serves society properly.

Together, these approaches create a complete strategy for handling AI's impact on society. Throughout the rest of this book we will utilize this Triple-Lens Framework to address the real AI ethics challenges we face today.

SECTION 2: USING EASTERN WISDOM TO ENSURE AI FAIRNESS

Traditional Western approaches to making algorithms fair are to treat everyone the same—that is, to give everyone equal opportunities and ensure equal results. While these solutions are *technically* correct, they often miss the bigger picture: what does it mean to be truly fair in diverse communities with changing needs?

Eastern philosophies offer an important viewpoint: instead of implementing algorithmic rules to be "equal," they emphasize developing good judgment and a complete understanding of how to build systems that are both unbiased and genuinely equitable. The following case study shows us how these ideas can work together in practice.

2.1 THREE KEY PHILOSOPHIES

- Supportive leadership: In Confucianism, it is emphasized that good leaders actively find ways to help people in society, especially those who are struggling. Leaders that simply follow rules and customs may be good managers, but they lack the proactive and empathetic vision to drive meaningful change. Considerate leadership also requires complete honesty about what one can and cannot do. For AI systems, this means that technology should be transparent about its limits and actively work to fix unfair treatment from the past.
- Daoist natural balance: Focusing on the natural flow of complex situations. Instead of forcing rigid solutions, recognize that things like fairness and efficiency are not enemies, but partners that need to be balanced. For AI, this means building systems that understand the real world and intuitively balance good performance with ethical outcomes.
- Clear rules: As Legalism states, good intentions aren't enough. You need strict, clear laws with real consequences. For AI, this means having strong regulations that demand fairness, with serious penalties for companies that don't comply.

2.2 CASE STUDY: IMPLEMENTING A HIRING ALGORITHM THROUGH THE TRIPLE-LENS FRAMEWORK

Consider the persistent issue of bias in hiring algorithms. A purely technical approach might focus solely on tweaking the algorithm to achieve statistical parity across demographic groups. Our framework, however, demands a more holistic strategy. The following five-pillar approach shows how these philosophies translate into concrete action, covering both internal cultivation and external enforcement.

Pillar 1: Cultivation of Virtual and Awareness

Before writing a single line of code, make sure the people building the system understand their own biases and blind spots. It's important to recognize that a tool is only as good as the hands and minds that build it.

- **In practice:** The team takes intensive workshops on recognizing bias. Encourage people from different backgrounds to share their job-hunting experiences and listen to how automated systems have affected them, both positively and negatively.

Pillar 2: Gather Data the Right Way

Carefully review old data to avoid repeating past microaggression. Actively seek out balanced information that reflects the real talent pool.

- **In practice:** Instead of scraping together historical data that carries with it past biases, proactively partner with universities and professional organizations in marginalized communities to build a more balanced dataset. Be completely upfront about how the data will be used and let people decide whether they want to participate or not.

Pillar 3: Build in the Open

Develop your algorithm in the open. Make the system's purpose and function clear to everyone. Let the design evolve based on continuous feedback from real people, not just the development team.

- **In practice:** Write the system's decision-making process in plain language that a non-expert could understand easily. Have an ethics review board with sociologists and worker advocates involved throughout development. Test the system with diverse groups before launching it.

Pillar 4: Keep Learning and Improving

Treat the system as something that needs constant attention and improvement, not a "set it and forget it" tool.

- **In practice:** Continue to monitor whether the algorithm treats different groups fairly or not. Create an easy way for rejected candidates to provide feedback for human review. Regularly update the system with new data to fix discovered problems.

Pillar 5: Combine Good Intentions with Firm Rules

Make sure that both the company culture and legal requirements work together to enforce accountability.

- **In practice:** Tie executive bonuses to meeting fairness goals, not just hiring speed. Make ethical decision-making a key part of performance reviews for your AI team. Consider going one step further by conducting strict external audits surrounding legal standards for fair algorithms. Support legislation that creates serious financial penalties for deceptive AI practices.

2.3 THE BIG PICTURE

Making AI fair is about building systems that work well technically, treat people ethically, and operate within clear legal boundaries. By combining these Eastern philosophical approaches, we can create technology that truly serves everyone in society.

SECTION 3: TRANSPARENCY AND ACCOUNTABILITY—THE LOOKING GLASS

3.1 THE PROBLEM WITH CURRENT APPROACHES

Most Western discussions regarding AI transparency are focused on giving people explanations when AI systems make decisions, as well as figuring out how to make complex computing models easier to understand. While these goals are important for data democracy, they often treat transparency like a set of technical problems to solve. Their solutions often involve creating tools to explain AI or checking compliance with rules.

Eastern philosophy offers a different way of thinking. Instead of asking how we can explain a system, it asks, "how can we build a system that naturally reflects the truth and builds trust?"

3.2 THREE KEY PHILOSOPHIES

- Confucian honesty and integrity: Transparency starts with good character. When organizations have clear consciences and strong ethics, they are naturally more open, as they have nothing to hide. Similarly, a system's function must match exactly what it claims to do. An algorithm can't call itself "neutral" if it actually works differently.
- Daoist simplicity: Overly complicated systems are usually fragmented ones. When you design something with a clear, sole purpose using simple principles, it becomes naturally easier to understand. Transparency is designed to stem naturally from good, simple design. It is not something you add on as an afterthought.
- Legalist rules and enforcement: As we mentioned in the previous section, there needs to be a counterbalance to virtue. On its own, it doesn't

make a strong enough impact. Legalism insists that standards must be clearly enforced. There must be measurable requirements for what companies have to disclose, to whom, and when. Most importantly, there needs to be a structured system to ensure compliance, creating unavoidable consequences for deception. This ensures that transparency is not a voluntary practice, but a non-negotiable requirement.

3.3 CASE STUDY: A CREDIT SCORING ALGORITHM DONE RIGHT

Let's take a look at how a bank might build a credit scoring algorithm. Instead of just giving people a reason for why they were denied a loan, this system contains five layers of transparency, each serving a different stakeholder group and purpose.

Layer 1: Intentional Transparency

The Bank Starts by Being Completely Honest About *Why* They Are Building This System.

- **In practice:** The bank publishes a clear statement claiming their algorithm's purpose is to help more people gain access to credit. They openly discuss the difficult choices involved, the potential for bias, and how they will measure the system's success beyond just looking at income.

Layer 2: Functional Transparency

The system actually works the way the bank claims it works.

- **In practice:** The application process is crystal clear. Instead of hiding behind technical jargon, it explains in simple terms what information is being used for. They also provide advice on what people can do to improve their credit (such as consistent bill payment). All marketing materials accurately describe what the system can and cannot do.

Layer 3: Procedural Transparency

The bank is completely open about their process, showing that their system development was thoroughly and ethically done.

- **In practice:** The company documents and shares how they test for racial and gender bias, how they clean their data, and how they handle customer complaints. They hire independent auditors and publish the results, proving that their methods are sound.

Layer 4: Algorithmic Transparency

The bank explains individual decisions clearly. When the system makes a decision regarding a loan, it provides a clear, helpful explanation.

- **In practice:** Instead of a confusing denial letter, someone might get a similar message to "Your application was declined because you have a short credit history and high recent spending in comparison to your income." This gives people real insight they can act upon.

Layer 5: Systemic Transparency

Understand the bigger picture. The bank recognizes that their algorithm doesn't exist in a vacuum. It affects entire communities and connects to historical inequalities.

- **In practice:** The bank funds research on how their algorithm affects different minorities, especially those that have faced discrimination in the past. They study whether they are actually helping to break cycles of disadvantage or unintentionally making them worse.

3.4 MAKING SURE IT ACTUALLY HAPPENS

Good intentions and smart design aren't impactful without enforcement. To ensure transparency:

- Set clear standards: Regulators should create strict rules about what counts as "adequate" transparency for each layer. They have the power to conduct surprise audits.
- Deliver real consequences: Implement fines for companies that violate transparency standards, along with personal liability for executives whose strategies intentionally deceive. This makes secrecy a catastrophic financial and legal risk.

3.5 PREVENTING MISUSE AND MALICIOUS ACTIONS

Beyond transparency, we need strong legal frameworks to prevent AI systems from being misused or designed with harmful intent. This is to make sure we proactively design systems to prevent harm before it happens.

1. **Controlling Who Can Access What**

   Misuse often happens because people don't understand a system's limits or because too many people have access to powerful tools.

- **In practice:** Many of the risks of misuse are covered by the GDPR, as well as the EU AI Act. That being said, companies still need to carefully manage API access to ensure partners only get the minimum amount of data needed for their specific tasks. Make sure every access request and query is automatically logged, creating a permanent record to track down improper use.
- **Legal requirements:** Companies must legally restrict access based on an employee's role and training level. Universal access to powerful AI tools is prohibited.[3]

2. **Severe Consequences so People Don't Risk It**
   The punishment for intentional misuse must be so certain that it effectively deters harmful behavior.
   - **In practice:** Highlight the fact that criminal charges will be issued for executives and developers that knowingly create systems designed to harm people. This encourages exposure of malicious projects early on.
   - **Real consequences:** Criminal liability holds executives personally responsible for their decisions.
3. **Rewarding Companies that Do the Right Thing**
   The system should actively encourage companies to identify and fix risks before they cause harm.
   - **In practice:** Companies get faster regulatory approval for voluntarily putting their systems through rigorous testing before launch. A bounty program can be put in place that reward ethical hackers and researchers for finding and reporting vulnerabilities that could lead to misuse.
   - **Incentives:** Make doing the right thing profitable, as opposed to just avoiding the wrong thing.

Altogether, this integrated approach ensures that transparency is an enforceable system of governance, protecting the good intentions of ethical companies from being exploited by bad actors.

3.6 THE BOTTOM LINE

True transparency goes beyond just explaining decisions after they are made. Great companies build systems that are honest, simple, and accountable from the ground up. By combining good character, smart design, and strong enforcement, we create AI systems that people can actually understand and trust.

SECTION 4: GOVERNANCE AND REGULATION—FINDING THE RIGHT BALANCE

4.1 THE PROBLEM TODAY

Most regions try to control AI with a plethora of detailed rules that protect individual rights and hold companies accountable. These goals are important, but this approach has problems. Some of the top issues are the following:

- Detailed rules quickly become outdated with fast-changing technology, slowing innovation while bad actors race ahead.
- Companies may choose compliance over substance, meaning that "checking boxes" is prioritized over genuine efforts to build ethical AI.
- The rule-heavy areas risk pushing AI research and development to less regulated regions. The problem is that smaller companies may not have the resources to comply, which leaves AI development in the hands of a select few tech giants.

The rule-heavy approach may protect individuals in the short term, but it slows progress and weakens competitiveness in the long term.

Eastern philosophy suggests a better way. Instead of trying to control everything from the top down, it emphasizes creating conditions where companies naturally want to do the right thing while still pursuing innovation.

4.2 THREE KEY PHILOSOPHIES

- **Confucian governance by virtue:** Good leadership matters most. The best governance comes from leaders with strong character; when leaders show integrity, care for others, and make wise decisions, it inspires everyone around them to act ethically too.
- **Daoist natural governance:** Effective governance should work with change, not fight against it. Good regulation should guide development toward helpful outcomes. Governance frameworks should feel organic and adaptive, not artificially rigid. The best governance involves taking necessary actions that yield the most harmonious outcome, with the least possible amount of forceful interference.

- **Legalist rule by clear law:** Good intentions need to be backed up with real consequences for doing harm, as well as meaningful rewards for exemplary practices. Ethical aspirations must be accompanied with tangible accountability.

4.3 WHY INDIVIDUAL RIGHTS AND THE PUBLIC INTEREST AREN'T OPPOSITES

One of the most significant contributions of Eastern philosophy to AI ethics is in its approach to balancing individual and collective interests. Western thinking often treats it as an either/or: either we protect individual privacy *or* we improve public safety. Eastern philosophy says this is wrong, as individual and collective well-being support each other.

The Confucian ideal of nesting levels of ethical development (see Figure 6.1) within each other (修身齐家治国平天下) basically tells us that

- Each decision that AI makes should be fair and understandable
- Each company should foster a culture that truly values doing right by people

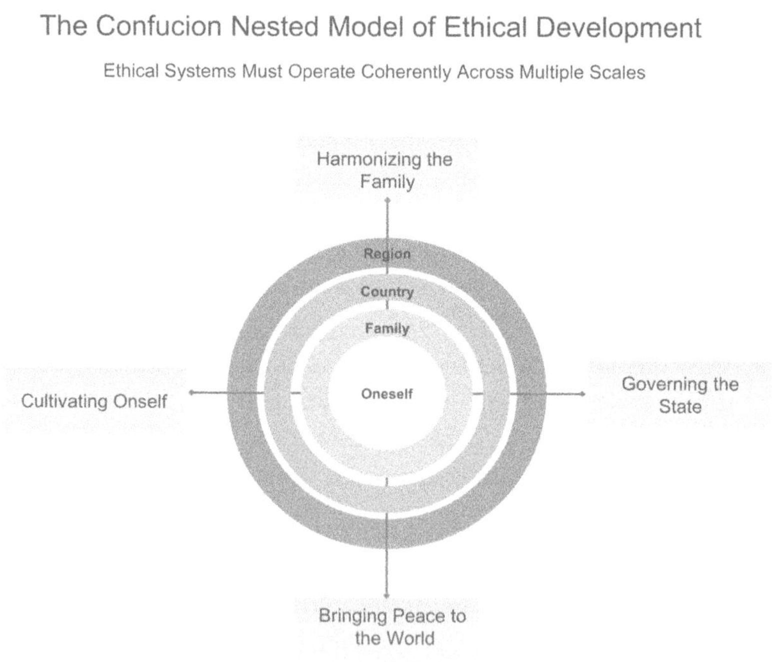

FIGURE 6.1 Nesting levels of ethical development.

- Each country should have rules that encourage innovation while protecting individuals
- Neighboring regions should create compatible laws so that technology benefits everyone, not just a select few players

This approach solves a key weakness in Western AI ethics: trying to solve individual problems (e.g. removing bias from a dataset) while ignoring the underlying issues that created the problems in the first place (e.g. the inequitable data collection practices of the entire industry). Eastern philosophy regards bias, transparency, and governance as intertwined aspects of a single ethical system, enabling holistic problem-solving approaches.

4.4 BUILDING ETHICAL TECHNOLOGY STARTS WITH THE PEOPLE

Eastern traditions place paramount importance on the cultivation of virtue as the foundation of ethical behavior. This view highlights something that strictly rule-based approaches to AI ethics often overlook. This virtue-based approach says that ethical technology must come from people with ethical principles themselves. Here is why this matters:

- Teaching awareness works better than just detecting problems: If developers truly understand bias and care about the people affected, they will find and fix problems that automated tools miss.
- Company culture beats compliance: A company that genuinely rewards ethical behavior will consistently do better than one that simply follows the minimum legal requirements.
- Real intentions create real results: People that truly want to build fair systems *will* build fair systems, not just systems that look fair on paper.

This changes the question from "how do we stop people from building harmful AI?" to "how do we systemically make people want to build helpful AI?"

4.5 THE GLOBAL CHALLENGE

AI doesn't respect borders. An algorithm trained in one country with data from around the world can affect people everywhere. This creates a nightmare for regulators who only have authority in their own countries.

The solution requires global cooperation based on a single principle: governance decisions should consider what benefits all of humanity, not just individual countries. Since every AI system depends on global collaboration, the governance of these systems has to be collaborative too.

4.6 CASE STUDY: REGULATING AI IN HEALTHCARE THROUGH THE "MIDDLE WAY"

Consider the challenge of governing AI in healthcare, where it's important to advance innovation in diagnostics and treatment while balancing risks to patient safety, privacy, and equity. A purely regulative approach might create a static checklist of compliance requirements that quickly become outdated. On the other hand, a completely non-formalistic approach would put patients at risk. Our approach, the "Middle Way," provides a dynamic balance between the two:

1. Adaptive regulatory systems: Rules that evolve with technology
   Instead of having fixed rules that become outdated quickly, create core principles that can adapt.

   - **In practice:** Regulators assign different risk levels for AI health tools. A scheduling app gets light oversight. A system that diagnoses cancer gets intensive review and continuous monitoring. The lessons learned from monitoring these tools are used to update guidance regularly, so that the rules grow with the technology.

2. Participatory oversight: Giving affected people real power
   The people directly affected by technology should help decide how it's governed.

   - **In practice:** Create a board of patients, caregivers, community health workers, and ethicists (not just technical experts) to review major decisions about AI in healthcare. This group advises on priorities and serves as a public forum for discussing real-world impacts.

3. International harmony: Countries working together
   Global problems need global solutions.

   - **In practice:** Companies in different regions agree on basic principles for medical AI (safety, effectiveness, fairness). They then accept each other's approvals for systems that meet these shared standards, while keeping the right to add their own specific requirements. This creates a cohesive list of principles to adhere to while respecting cultural differences.

4. Legalist enforcement of lines not to cross
   A flexible system needs a foundation of absolute rules with severe consequences.

   - **In practice:** Executives face charges if they knowingly deploy dangerous, uncertified medical AI. Companies pay massive fines for violating privacy or creating biased systems that harm minorities. This Legalist foundation ensures that having ethical practices is not a path of weakness, but one of disciplined balance.

4.7 WHY THE MIDDLE WAY IS EFFECTIVE

This balanced approach creates an ecosystem where companies want to do the right thing because it benefits their business, while unethical behavior has consequences serious enough to actually deter it. Innovation can flourish within clear boundaries, and rules can evolve as technology changes. Instead of an endless arms race between rule-makers and rule-breakers, this approach creates conditions where ethical behavior naturally emerges and spreads throughout the industry.

SECTION 5: PUTTING IT ALL TOGETHER—A COMPLETE FRAMEWORK FOR ETHICAL AI

5.1 WHY COMBINING EAST WITH WEST WORKS BETTER

The integration of Eastern philosophical principles with Western AI ethics creates a more complete approach to responsible AI development. This doesn't mean throwing out Western approaches. It just means strengthening them with insights from Eastern traditions.

The character foundation: Eastern philosophy maintains that ethical technology comes from inherently ethical people and organizations. Simply following rules is not going to be enough. You need to actively build good character. This means ongoing moral education for AI practitioners, company cultures that genuinely reward doing the right thing, and leaders who demonstrate a real commitment to public welfare.

The balance principle: Instead of viewing difficult choices as win–lose situations, Eastern thinking looks for creative solutions that serve multiple groups simultaneously. This involves bringing diverse perspectives into AI development, actively seeking out solutions where everyone benefits, and creating governance that both protects people and enables innovation.

The adaptive wisdom approach: Eastern philosophy places an emphasis on applying practical wisdom to long-term goals, rather than just focusing on technical expertise. This means flexible governance that can evolve with technology, continuous learning from real-world results, and collaboration between technical experts and people who understand social impacts.

5.2 NEW IMPLEMENTATION GUIDELINES

Here is a set of specific actions that go beyond what we've already discussed.

For AI developers and teams:

1. Cultivate ethical character
    - Regularly reflect on personal biases and assumptions
    - Participate in ongoing education concerning AI ethics and social impacts
    - Develop empathy through direct engagement with affected communities
    - Practice mindfulness and contemplative techniques to increase awareness
2. Implement harmonious development processes
    - Create multidisciplinary teams that include ethicists to balance innovation with responsibility
    - Design systems that complement rather than replace human judgment
    - Prioritize solutions that serve multiple stakeholder interests concurrently
3. Embrace adaptive governance
    - Develop flexible architecture that can be modified as understanding evolves
    - Implement continuous monitoring and evaluation systems

- Create rapid response mechanisms for addressing problems
- Establish clear protocols for learning from failures

For organizations:

1. Develop virtue-based leadership
    - Select leaders who demonstrate a genuine commitment to ethical behavior
    - Provide ongoing ethical education for executives and managers
    - Integrate ethical considerations into strategic planning and decision-making
    - Create accountability mechanisms that encourage ethical behavior
2. Foster a collaborative culture
    - Encourage open dialogue surrounding ethical challenges and dilemmas
    - Create safe spaces for raising concerns about AI systems and their impacts
    - Develop partnerships with affected communities and stakeholders
3. Implement comprehensive transparency
    - Provide clear, accessible information about AI systems and their purposes
    - Establish regular reports on AI performance and social impacts
    - Create meaningful mechanisms for stakeholder input and feedback
    - Be honest about limitations, uncertainties, and potential consequences

For policymakers:

1. Develop adaptive regulatory frameworks
    - Create flexible regulations that can evolve alongside technological development
    - Establish clear principles while allowing for diverse implementation approaches

- Include mechanisms for the consistent review and updating of regulations

2. Promote virtue-based governance
   - Select public officials who demonstrate a genuine commitment to public welfare
   - Provide ongoing education of AI technology and its social implications
   - Create incentives for responsible AI development and deployment
   - Model ethical behavior at the leadership level when using AI systems
3. Ensure meaningful participation
   - Establish accessible mechanisms for public input on AI governance
   - Include diverse voices in AI policy development processes
   - Provide resources for community organizations to engage with AI issues
   - Create ongoing dialogue between technologists, policymakers, and affected communities

For citizens and civil society:

1. Cultivate AI literacy
   - Learn about AI technology and its social implications
   - Develop critical thinking skills for evaluating AI claims and promises
   - Stay informed about AI developments and their potential impacts
2. Practice active engagement
   - Participate in public discussions surrounding AI governance and regulation
   - Advocate for transparency and accountability in AI systems that affect your community

- Support organizations and leaders who prioritize ethical AI development
- Hold institutions accountable for their AI practices and policies

3. Foster community wisdom
    - Share knowledge and experiences about AI impacts with others
    - Organize community discussions regarding AI ethics and governance
    - Collaborate with other communities facing similar challenges
    - Contribute to research and advocacy on ethical issues

5.3 HOW TO MEASURE REAL PROGRESS

Eastern philosophy emphasizes cultivation and continuous improvement rather than fixed achievements. Here is how to track whether or not we are actually making progress toward ethical AI.

Early warning indicators

- Increasing complexity in AI explanations often means systems are becoming less accountable
- Growing gaps between AI performance for different demographic groups indicates emerging bias issues
- A rising number of "AI incidents" that surprise developers suggests insufficient ethical preparation

Positive progress markers

- AI developers can clearly explain not just how their systems work, but why they made specific choices
- Regulatory frameworks evolve smoothly with technology rather than always lagging behind
- International cooperation on AI ethics increases rather than fragmenting into competing approaches

The goal isn't perfection. We want to build systems and cultures that are capable of continuous ethical evolution as both technology and our understanding of its impacts continue to develop.

CONCLUSION: THE ONGOING JOURNEY OF ETHICAL AI

Combining Eastern wisdom with Western AI ethics offers a pathway toward more humane and effective use of artificial intelligence. By learning from ancient philosophical traditions, we can better understand what it means to develop technology that truly serves people.

These insights don't replace Western approaches at all. Rather, they make them stronger and more complete. The result is a framework that addresses not only technical problems but also the human side of AI development. This approach recognizes that ethical AI requires better people, organizations, and societies, as opposed to just better algorithms.

Ethical AI is an ongoing journey we must navigate together. We need wisdom from both the East and West, honesty in acknowledging our limitations, and an unwavering commitment to helping all people thrive. The path toward ethical AI is not easy but is worth taking because it leads us to a future where technology serves humanity's best interests.

NOTES

1. "Merseyside Police: AI Used to Detect Driving Offences." *BBC*, 2023, bbc.com/news/uk-england-merseyside-67365823.
2. Martineau, Kim. "Shrinking Deep Learning's Carbon Footprint." *Massachusetts Institute of Technology*, 2020, news.mit.edu/2020/shrinking-deep-learning-carbon-footprint-0807.
3. "High-Level Summary of the AI Act." *EU Artificial Intelligence Act*, 2024, artificialintelligenceact.eu/high-level-summary/.

CHAPTER 7

Leadership in the Age of AI

The New Rules of Success

> The wise leader is like water. Water nourishes all things and does not compete.
>
> —LAO TZU[1]

Without a doubt, artificial intelligence (AI) is changing how we work. More importantly, it is fundamentally reshaping who holds power and how they use it. The era of command and control leadership is ending. The leaders that thrive won't be the loudest in the room or the most aggressive personalities. They'll be the ones who understand a deeper principle: that the best leaders don't fight against change but guide it instead.

Here is the truth: AI doesn't make human leadership obsolete. In fact, it matters more than ever. Machines can optimize, predict, and execute. But they can't inspire. They can't foster trust. They can't navigate the unseen currents of culture, ethics, and meaning. That's your role. So it isn't a question of how to control technology, but rather:

> How do I lead in a world where power belongs to those who can inspire and guide, rather than command and control?

DOI: 10.1201/9781003644699-7

SECTION 1: THE CHANGING OF LEADERSHIP THROUGH EASTERN EYES

The leadership world is truly undergoing a profound transformation, driven largely by AI. It is completely changing what it means to truly lead. AI is reshaping how decisions are made, how teams are guided, and how organizations navigate the path to success.

Consider this: leaders now have direct access to real-time data and automated processes. This means they can make smarter, faster, and more strategic decisions than ever before. It's a game changer, allowing them to step back from the daily grind and really concentrate on fostering innovation, developing their people, and building adaptable, welcoming cultures.

But it's not all straightforward. The rise of AI brings significant challenges with it. Leaders need to thoughtfully address complex ethical questions, safeguard data privacy, and make sure AI is used in a way that is both responsible and transparent. The leaders that will experience the most success are those who can comfortably blend their technical fluency with strong emotional intelligence, adaptability, and a genuine focus on human values. When human creativity and machine intelligence work together like this, we can expect to see extraordinary results.

For ages, foreign philosophies have offered profound insights that Western business culture often dismissed as impractical idealism. In the Hindu concept of dharma, there exists a profound understanding that each being has a unique purpose that contributes to the cosmic order.[2] Similarly, in the age of AI, leaders must recognize that their role is not to compete with AI, but to fulfill their distinct duty, which is to provide the experience, empathy, and moral guidance that no algorithm can replicate.

The Japanese principle of ikigai, which in a professional context represents the convergence of what you love, what you're good at, what the world needs, and what you can be paid for,[3] becomes particularly relevant as AI transforms job markets and organizational structures. Leaders must help their teams discover their ikigai in an AI-augmented world, aligning their passions and strengths with meaningful work that creates value beyond automation.

Traditional command and control structures, built on the assumption of information scarcity and centralized knowledge, crumble in the face of AI systems that can process and analyze data faster than any human team. The Daoist concept of Yin and Yang offers a framework for understanding this transition: the Yang energy of assertive, top–down leadership must balance with the Yin component of receptive, collaborative guidance.

Leaders become orchestrators of the dance between human intuition and AI, creating an overall balance between the two.

The African philosophy of Ubuntu ("I am because we are")[4] gives us another point of view on AI-driven organizations. Ubuntu highlights the fact that individual success is meaningless without collective prosperity. In AI-integrated workplaces, this means that we have to ensure technological advancement serves not just efficiency metrics, but also the collective benefit of all stakeholders. While AI optimizes our work, a leader's role is to ensure it also strengthens the relationships that give that work meaning.

SECTION 2: THE ESSENTIAL SKILLS FOR LEADING IN TOMORROW'S WORLD

The master of any art avoids excess and defect.

—ARISTOTLE[5]

CEOs are often unable to explain why their company's AI initiative has failed spectacularly. They invested millions of dollars in cutting-edge technology, hired top-notch data scientists, and implemented systems that were technically impressive. Clearly, technology is not the issue—so what goes wrong?

The answer lies in leadership and human intelligence. Oftentimes, companies focus on the AI aspect and place governance on the back-burner, which causes a major rift between their technology and their people. Executives make the mistake of applying old frameworks to entirely new scenarios, still attempting to "manage" AI projects and "integrate" AI tactics as opposed to fundamentally ingraining AI into their business. Employing an improper mindset leads to directionless and, more often than not, unsuccessful AI projects.[6]

This principle has stuck with me because it captures something crucial about this point in history. We are so focused on understanding AI that we sometimes forget that human intelligence is a key part of the equation. The truth is, leading in the age of AI isn't about becoming a technical expert at all. It's about developing a new set of human capabilities that complement and guide our technological tools.

After working with dozens of organizations navigating AI transformation, I've identified seven core competencies (see Figure 7.1) that separate leaders who thrive in the AI era from those who struggle. These aren't technical skills you can learn from a coding workshop. They are deeper capabilities that draw on the age-old fundamentals of human nature,

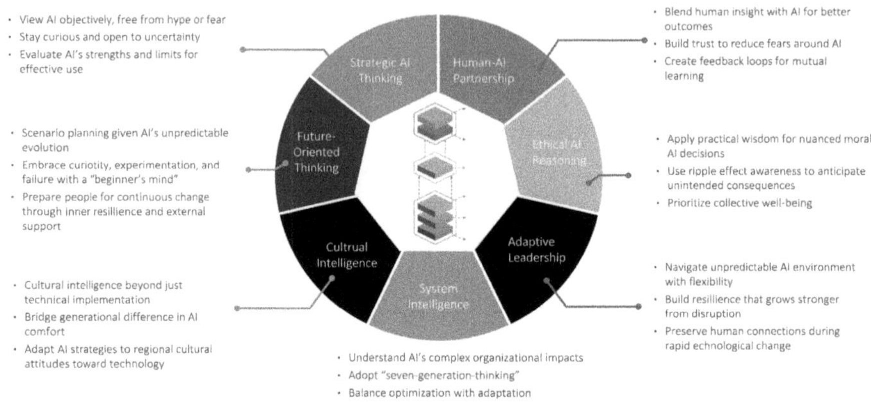

FIGURE 7.1 Seven essential leadership skills.

decision-making, and relationships. These are the skills that will become more and more important as machines get smarter.

2.1 COMPETENCY 1: STRATEGIC AI THINKING

Beyond the Hype and Fear

The first competency is strategic AI thinking. It is the ability to see AI clearly, without getting caught up in either the hype or the panic. This sounds simple enough, but in reality, we are bombarded daily with stories about AI that claim it will either solve all our problems or destroy civilization. Neither narrative is particularly helpful when you are trying to make practical decisions about how to use AI in your organization.

Strategic AI thinking starts with what Buddhist philosophy calls "clear seeing," which is the ability to observe reality without the distortion of our hopes, fears, or preconceptions.[7] When working with company leaders, I often ask them to describe their relationship with AI. The answers are revealing. Some see it as a magical transformative force for their business, whereas others view it as a threat that will render them obsolete. Both perspectives make it nearly impossible to make well-informed decisions.

The leaders that excel at strategic AI thinking have learned to hold what Zen Buddhism calls the "not-knowing mind." It refers to a comfortable uncertainty that allows them to remain curious and open to learning.[8] They see AI as an opportunity for growth, not a concept to be memorized. These leaders are able to objectively weigh AI's unique strengths and weaknesses and apply them to specific, well-defined problems, which is where it works best.

Understanding Interconnectedness

Strategic AI thinking also requires the ability to see the big picture—how a change in one part of the company affects all the others. This mirrors the ancient Chinese concept of "Wu Xing," the theory of the five elements, which describes how different aspects of a system influence each other in complex and often unnoticeable ways.

When you implement AI into customer service, it doesn't just affect *your* call center. It also changes how customers interact with your brand, how employees feel about their work, how your competitors respond, and how your community views your company. Strategic AI thinkers map out these connections before making important decisions.

Consider a retail CEO that wants to use AI for inventory management. Instead of focusing only on the efficiency gains, she considers the broader implications. How will this affect relationships with suppliers? What will happen to employees whose jobs involve handling inventory decisions? How might this change the shopping experience for customers? By thinking systemically, she is able to implement AI in a way that creates value for all stakeholders, not just the bottom line.

The pace of AI development makes it impossible to predict exactly how technology will evolve, but leaders can develop principles and frameworks that help them adapt to whatever comes next.

2.2 COMPETENCY 2: ORCHESTRATING THE HUMAN–AI PARTNERSHIP

The Art of Partnership

The second essential skill is proficiency in human–AI collaboration. This goes far beyond simply knowing how to use AI tools. It's about knowing how to best combine human judgment with machine power for superior results.

Human intelligence and AI have complementary qualities: humans excel at creativity, empathy, ethical reasoning, and contextual understanding, while AI excels at pattern recognition, data processing, speed, and consistency. The secret is taking the strengths of each and putting them together.

Creating Feedback Loops

Effective human–AI collaboration thrives on kaizen, the Japanese principle of continuous improvement. It entails creating feedback loops where humans and AI systems learn from each other over time.

This is different from traditional training, where you learn something once and then apply it. With human–AI collaboration, both parties are constantly adapting. AI learns from human corrections and insights, while humans learn to better understand AI's capabilities and limitations.

A manufacturing company I worked with created an AI apprenticeship program, where experienced workers partnered with AI systems to optimize production processes. Employees would point out factors that didn't show up in the data, such as how weather affects equipment performance or how employee morale impacts quality. At the same time, AI would help humans see patterns they might have missed and would figure out the most efficient way to utilize time and resources.

Over time, this partnership became incredibly sophisticated. The workers developed an intuition regarding when to trust AI recommendations and when to override them. The AI system became more accurate by incorporating human insights that could not be learnt through the rulebook alone. Most importantly, the employees felt like partners in the process rather than people being replaced by it.

Managing the Emotional Dimension

Working with AI requires an understanding of how people feel about it. Leaders need to be adept at addressing their team's fears, building trust, and channeling excitement productively.

It's completely normal for people to be scared of AI. They worry it will render their jobs obsolete, that it will make mistakes they'll be blamed for, or that it will dehumanize their work. These are natural responses to significant change.

Leaders with collaboration fluency don't dismiss these concerns or try to brush them off through logical explanation. Instead, they create spaces for people to express their feelings and work through them. They share their own uncertainties and the learning process they went through. They celebrate examples of successful human–AI partnership and help their coworkers develop confidence in their ability to work with AI effectively.

2.3 COMPETENCY 3: ETHICAL AI REASONING—NAVIGATING MORAL COMPLEXITIES

Beyond Rules and Compliance

The third competency is ethical AI reasoning: the skill to navigate moral dilemmas when AI impacts human lives. This goes far beyond following compliance rules or an ethical checklist. It requires the kind of deep moral reasoning that philosophers have spent thousands of years developing.

This is where the ancient Greek concept of phronesis becomes essential. It encompasses the practical wisdom to make ethical judgments in nuanced situations, considering relationships and consequences, not just rules.[9] For example, it distinguishes knowing that lying is wrong from knowing when using blunt truth could be more harmful than beneficial.

AI decisions often involve this type of nuanced moral reasoning. For example, when an AI system recommends laying off certain employees to optimize efficiency, a leader needs to consider not just the economic logic but also the human impact, the message it sends to employees, the effect on families and communities, and the long-term impact on the organization.

These are the questions AI cannot answer. They required a balance of human wisdom, field expertise, ethics, and awareness of what matters to the community. This is why we need practical wisdom to guide leaders through these decisions, where there is no clear right or wrong, but certainly life-changing outcomes on either end.

Coming Across Unintended Consequences

Ethical AI reasoning also requires what Buddhist philosophy calls "dependent origination," which helps us see how our actions ripple through complex systems and affect people we might never meet.[10]

AI systems often have effects that go far beyond their intended purpose. A hiring algorithm, trained on historical data, designed to find the best candidates for a position could unintentionally discriminate against certain groups. A recommendation system designed to show people content they'll enjoy might create echo chambers that polarize society. A predictive policing system designed to prevent crime might reinforce racial biases in law enforcement.

This is why it is crucial to practice "ripple effect awareness," which is essentially the habit of asking not just "will this work?", but also "who might be affected by this?", "what could go wrong here?", and "what precedent are we setting?"

A tech executive I worked with was considering implementing an AI system to monitor employee productivity. The system would track keystrokes, mouse movements, and application usage to identify when people were being less productive. From a narrow efficiency perspective, it made sense. But when she applied ripple effect thinking, she realized the system would fundamentally change the culture of trust in her organization, potentially driving away their best employees and creating an atmosphere of surveillance and fear.

Instead, she focused on using AI to actually help employees be more productive through tools that could automate routine tasks, provide insights about work patterns, and suggest ways to improve workflows. Same technology, completely different application resulted in dramatically different impact on human flourishing.

Balancing Stakeholder Interests

The Ubuntu philosophy teaches us that individual and community well-being are interconnected in a way that you cannot have one without the other. This wisdom becomes crucial when making ethical decisions surrounding AI implementation.

Modern business often focuses on shareholder value, but ethical AI reasoning requires considering all stakeholders: employees, customers, surrounding communities, and future generations. This doesn't mean you aren't allowed to make a profit, or that every decision must make everyone happy. It means you consider the full impact of your choices and look for solutions that serve multiple stakeholders rather than benefitting one group at the expense of others.

2.4 COMPETENCY 4: ADAPTIVE LEADERSHIP IN UNCERTAINTY—THRIVING IN THE UNKNOWN

Embracing the Unknowable

The fourth competency is adaptive leadership, which refers to the ability to guide organizations through periods of uncertainty and rapid change. The AI era is characterized by what military strategists call the "VUCA" condition: volatility, uncertainty, complexity, and ambiguity.[11] Traditional leadership approaches that rely on detailed planning and predictable outcomes don't work well in this environment.

The I Ching, an ancient Chinese text, is essentially a manual for leading in uncertain times. It teaches that change is the only constant and that wisdom lies in learning to flow with change rather than fighting against it. This doesn't mean being passive or reactive; it means developing the sensitivity to read emerging patterns, and the agility to adapt your approach as circumstances shift.

Imagine a CEO whose industry is being disrupted by AI-powered competitors. His natural instinct is to create a detailed five-year plan for AI adoption. But every month, new developments in AI capabilities make parts of his plan obsolete. Instead of getting frustrated, he learns to focus on being clear about his overall objective, while staying flexible about tactics.

His new approach involves setting clear principles like "we will use AI to serve customers better, not to eliminate jobs." He also created small experiments to test different approaches. When an experiment worked, the approach was scaled up. When it didn't, they learned from it and kept trying from a different angle. This iterative approach allowed them to adapt quickly to changing conditions while maintaining a sense of direction and purpose.

Building Resilient Organizations

A key part of adaptive leadership is creating resilience, that is, the ability to handle major disruptions while staying true to who you are. For AI transformation, this means being able to navigate technology changes without losing sight of your organization's core values.

The concept of antifragility is relevant here. It refers to systems that don't just survive stress but actually get stronger from it. Organizations with this quality use AI disruption as an opportunity to become more innovative, more connected to their purpose, and more responsive to customer needs.

This requires what I call "distributed leadership"—developing leadership capabilities throughout the organization rather than concentrating them at the top. When change is happening rapidly, you need people at every level who can make well-informed decisions, adapt to new circumstances, and help others navigate uncertainty.

What this looks like: instead of having AI decisions made only by senior executives, a manufacturing company trains supervisors and team leaders to understand AI capabilities and make implementation decisions for their sectors. This distributed approach allows them to adapt much more quickly to changing conditions and helps employees feel more involved in the transformation process.

Maintaining Human Connection in Digital Transformation

Perhaps most importantly, adaptive leadership in the AI era requires maintaining human connection and learning even as technology changes how work gets done. External changes are inevitable, but it's important that our core values and unique contributions remain consistent, especially as job roles change rapidly.

This involves establishing "rituals of continuity," a practice to help people stay connected to their purpose even as everything else shifts around them. The method of implementation is quite flexible: it might be regular check-ins where people share how they're feeling about the changes, or it might be storytelling sessions where people share examples of how their work makes a difference.

2.5 COMPETENCY 5: SYSTEM INTELLIGENCE—NAVIGATING INTERCONNECTED NETWORKS

Seeing How Everything Connects

The fifth competency is having intelligence regarding systems: the ability to understand complex relationships and interdependencies between these systems rather than focusing on isolated events or individual components. This capability becomes crucial in the AI era because AI implementation affects multiple aspects of an organization simultaneously, and often in unexpected ways.

Traditional Silicon Valley thinking tends to be linear. For example, if A causes B, then doing more of A will produce more of B. Systems thinking, on the other hand, recognizes that complex systems behave in non-linear ways. Small changes can have compounding effects, and large efforts can sometimes produce no change at all.

A hospital wants to use AI to reduce patient wait times in their emergency department. A linear approach would have focused on the AI system itself, which is how fast it could process patient information, how accurately it could predict treatment times, and how efficiently it could allocate resources. Instead, they applied systems thinking, mapping out all the factors that could potentially affect wait times: staffing levels, equipment availability, communication between departments. Even factors like weather and local events were considered. They realized that implementing AI without addressing these interconnected factors would be like trying to bake a cake with the wrong ingredients.

Alternatively, they used AI as part of a broader systems approach. It was able to help with resource allocation and prediction but also improved communication protocols and created better relationships with other healthcare providers in the region. The result was a dramatic reduction in wait times and a more resilient system overall.

Seeing Patterns Across Time

Systems thinking also involves what Indigenous cultures call "seven-generation thinking," which is to consider how our actions today will affect a system seven generations into the future.[12] This long-term perspective becomes crucial when implementing AI systems that will shape the organizational culture and capabilities for years to come.

Many AI implementations focus on immediate efficiency gains without considering long-term effects on employee skills, organizational learning, or competitive positioning. A systems-thinking leader asks questions like the following: "What capabilities are we building or losing?" "How will this change our relationship with customers?" "What precedent are we setting for future decisions?"

Balancing Optimization and Adaptation

Systems thinking also requires an understanding of the tension between optimization and adaptation. AI is incredibly good at optimizing existing processes, or in other words, finding the most efficient way to achieve current objectives. But overoptimization can make systems fragile and less able to adapt to changing conditions.

This reflects the Daoist principle that action should flow naturally rather than forcing outcomes. Sometimes the most efficient solution in the short term creates problems in the long term. Sometimes maintaining some room for improvement makes a system more resilient and adaptable.

2.6 COMPETENCY 6: CULTURAL INTELLIGENCE—BRIDGING THE HUMAN AND DIGITAL WORLDS

Understanding Cultural Dynamics

The sixth competency is cultural intelligence: the ability to understand and navigate the cultural dimensions of AI implementation. Every organization has its own culture, and AI implementation either reinforces or changes that culture in significant ways. Leaders need to be intentional about which cultural elements they want to preserve, and which they want to evolve.

This requires what anthropologists call "thick description," which means understanding not just what people do, but why they do it, what it means to them, and how it connects to their sense of identity and belonging.[13] When you implement AI, you are not just changing processes; you are potentially redefining what it means to work at your organization.

I visited a professional services firm that prided itself on the craft and expertise of its consultants. They were considering implementing AI to automate much of the research and analysis that junior consultants typically did. From an efficiency perspective, it made perfect sense. But from a cultural perspective, it threatened to undermine their apprenticeship model and the path through which people developed industry expertise.

The solution required cultural intelligence. Instead of simply automating their junior work, they redesigned roles so that AI handled routine research while junior consultants focused on client interaction, creative problem-solving, and learning from senior colleagues. This preserved the cultural elements that were important to the organization while still making practical use of the benefits of AI.

Bridging Generational Perspectives

Cultural intelligence involves understanding how different generations relate to AI and technology in different ways. Younger employees might be more comfortable with AI tools but lack the experience to know when to question AI recommendations. Older employees have more wisdom regarding business contexts but may be less comfortable with exploring new technologies.

The key is creating what the Korean concept of 정 ("jeong") describes: emotional connections that transcend individual differences.[14] This means finding ways for different generations to learn from each other rather than seeing generational differences as a gap to bridge.

An example of this is reverse mentoring programs where younger employees teach older workers how to use AI tools, while older employees share their knowledge about production processes, quality control, and customer relationships. This approach honors the wisdom of both groups while building the collaborative culture needed for successful AI implementation.

Managing Change Across Cultures

For global organizations, cultural intelligence means understanding how AI implementation affects attitude toward authority, individual vs. collective decision-making, the role of technology in society, and concepts of privacy and surveillance, all of which vary significantly across different cultures.

What works in one cultural context may not work in another, and leaders need to adapt their approach accordingly. This doesn't mean having completely different AI strategies for different regions, but it does mean being sensitive to cultural factors in how you implement, communicate, and manage AI systems.

2.7 COMPETENCY 7: FUTURE-ORIENTED THINKING—PREPARING FOR WHAT'S NEXT

Scenario Planning with Humility

The seventh and final competency is future-oriented thinking, which is the ability to prepare for several possible outcomes rather than betting everything on a single prediction. Given the rapid pace of AI development, it is impossible to know exactly how technology will evolve, but leaders can develop the capability to adapt to various scenarios on the go.

This requires what the ancient Greeks called "sophia," which is a type of wisdom that combines knowledge with humility about the limits of one's knowledge.[15] Future-oriented leaders stay informed about AI developments but avoid the trap of thinking they can predict exactly how things will unfold.

Building Learning Organizations

Future-oriented thinking also requires building what Peter Senge calls "learning organizations." Those are the organizations that can adapt and evolve as conditions change. This means creating cultures that value curiosity, experimentation, and learning from failure.[16]

The Buddhist concept of beginner's mind becomes essential here. Organizations that approach AI with an open mindset are more likely to discover unexpected applications, avoid dangerous assumptions, and adapt quickly to new developments.

This means creating structures and processes that support ongoing learning: regular experiments with new AI tools, cross-functional teams that share insights across departments, and time allocated for employees to explore and learn.

Preparing People for Continuous Change

Finally, future-oriented thinking requires preparing people psychologically and emotionally for a world of continuous change. The traditional career model of learning skills once and being able to apply them for decades is being replaced by a model of continuous learning and adaptation.

Leaders play a pivotal role in helping employees develop a sense of inner resilience, while also providing the external support, such as training, resources, and community, that makes continuous adaptation possible.

SECTION 3: PUTTING IT ALL TOGETHER—THE INTEGRATED LEADER

The Confucian concept of "ren (仁)," often translated as benevolence or humaneness, encompasses the qualities that will distinguish human leaders in the AI era. More than just kindness, ren involves a deep understanding of human nature and social relationships. As AI systems excel at pattern recognition and optimization, leaders must excel at recognizing the patterns of human motivation, the optimization of team dynamics, and the complex notions of trust and inspiration.

The seven competencies mentioned in this chapter don't exist in isolation. They work together to create an integrated leadership framework for the age of AI. Leaders who facilitate human–AI collaboration also need cultural intelligence to understand what collaboration means in different contexts. Leaders who think systemically also need future-oriented thinking to understand how systems evolve over time.

The Daoist concept of "wu wei (无为)," often translated as "non-action," is better described as action that flows naturally from fully understanding a situation.[17] When leaders develop all seven competencies, their actions flow more naturally, stemming from a complete understanding of the complex environment they are navigating.

This doesn't mean leadership becomes effortless. It means it becomes more skillful and deliberate. Like a martial artist who has been practicing for decades, the movements become more fluid and effective through deep understanding and practice.

The path to developing these competencies isn't quick or easy. But for leaders willing to do the work, the AI era offers unprecedented opportunities to create organizations that are more effective, more humane, and more adaptable than anything we have seen before.

NOTES

1. Lao Tzu, "Lao Tzu quotes." C770–C481 BC, *The Wisest Words*, thewisestwords.com/lau-tzu-quotes/.
2. The Dharma Devotee, "Basic Concepts of Hinduism." *Compass Wisdom*, 2025, compasswisdom.com/Basic-Concepts-of-Hinduism.
3. "Ikigai." *Johns Hopkins University*, imagine.jhu.edu/resources/ikigai/.
4. Marshall, Vicky. "What's in a Word? The Meaning of Ubuntu." *The Dandelion Philosophy*, 2025, dandelionphilosophy.com/blog/whats-in-a-word-the-meaning-of-ubuntu.

5. Aristotle, "Nicomachean Ethics by Aristotle." 384–322 BC, *Boston University*, translated by W. D. Ross, people.bu.edu/wwildman/courses/wphil/readings/wphil_rdg09_nichomacheanethics_entire.htm.
6. Joshi, Sandeep. "The AI Leadership Crisis—Why Smart Leaders Are Abandoning Traditional Transformation." *Medium*, 2025, sandeepmvp.medium.com/the-ai-leadership-crisis-why-smart-leaders-are-abandoning-traditional-transformation-18fcda152699.
7. Wisdomlib, "Pure Seeing: Significance and Symbolism." *Wisdom Library*, 2025, wisdomlib.org/concept/pure-seeing.
8. Hartman, Zenkei Blanche. "The Zen of Not Knowing." *Tricycle: The Buddhist Review*, 2022, tricycle.org/article/zen-not-knowing/.
9. Sheposh, Richard. "Phronesis." *Elton B. Stephens Company*, 2021, ebsco.com/research-starters/religion-and-philosophy/phronesis.
10. "The Principle of Interdependence in Buddhism: Dependent Origination." *Philosophy Institute*, 2023, philosophy.institute/religions-of-the-world/dependent-origination-buddhism-interdependence/.
11. Wright, Gavin, and Ivy Wigmore. "What Is VUCA (Volatility, Uncertainty, Complexity and Ambiguity)?" *TechTarget*, 2023, techtarget.com/whatis/definition/VUCA-volatility-uncertainty-complexity-and-ambiguity.
12. "What Is the Seventh Generation Principle?" *Indigenous Corporate Training Inc.*, 2020, ictinc.ca/blog/seventh-generation-principle.
13. McLeod, Saul. "Thick Description in Qualitative Research." *SimplyPsychology*, 2024, reviewed by Olivia Guy-Evans, simplypsychology.org/thick-description.html.
14. Rayner, Gabii. "The Korean Concept of 'Jeong'." *Cherry Chu Magazine*, 2022, cherrychumagazine.com/entertainment/the-korean-concept-of-jeong.
15. Selfsutras. "The Wisdom of Unknowing: Exploring Socratic Humility, Upanishadic Knowledge, and Mystical Insight." *Medium*, 2024, medium.com/%40selfsutras/the-wisdom-of-unknowing-exploring-socratic-humility-upanishadic-knowledge-and-mystical-insight-ee02e5bbb7ca.
16. Lannon, Colleen. "Learning Organizations: From Invention to Innovation." *The Systems Thinker*, 2018, thesystemsthinker.com/learning-organizations-from-invention-to-innovation/.
17. Lark Editor Team. "Wu Wei: The Art of Effortless Action." *Lark*, 2023, larksuite.com/en_us/topics/productivity-glossary/wu-wei.

CHAPTER 8

The Global AI Landscape

Innovations, Policies, and Cultural Perspectives

SECTION 1: THE UNEVEN TERRAIN OF GLOBAL AI ADOPTION

Artificial intelligence (AI) is reshaping societies worldwide, but its influence emerges at different speeds depending on where you look. While Silicon Valley narratives suggest that AI transformation is universal, the reality is far more disconnected. Whether in Shenzhen's tech hubs, Bangalore's startup networks, or Stockholm's research labs, AI is being developed, deployed, and governed in completely different ways.

The myth surrounding uniform AI progress suggests that technology follows a predictable path from innovation to adoption. The global reality tells a very different yet intriguing story: AI is being shaped by local contexts as much as it is shaping them (see Figure 8.1). Geography, culture, and economics determine what problems AI is asked to solve, how success is measured, and what kind of tradeoffs are considered acceptable.

Understanding these differences is especially important for leaders navigating the global economy. They need to be able to recognize how AI adoption varies across cultures, as the strategies that work in one context may fail spectacularly in another. The regulatory assumptions that guide

DOI: 10.1201/9781003644699-8

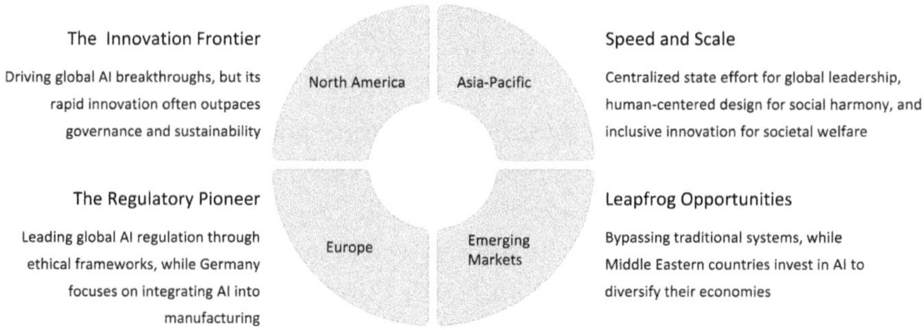

FIGURE 8.1 Regional variations in AI adoption.

decisions in one market may be completely invalid in another. The cultural values that make certain AI applications acceptable in one society may make them unthinkable elsewhere.

As we look at how AI is developing around the world, we will see that no single country or company is determining its future. Instead, AI's prospects are being shaped by many things happening simultaneously: local innovation, global competition, cultural wisdom, and regular experimentation, which all dictate how AI gets used. Governments today are also trying to enforce different rules and regulations on this technology.

The leaders who can see both the forest and the trees of global AI development will be the ones best able to take advantage of opportunities and handle problems as they arise.

SECTION 2: REGIONAL VARIATIONS IN AI ADOPTION

2.1 NORTH AMERICA: THE INNOVATION FRONTIER

Silicon Valley's Gravitational Pull

Silicon Valley remains the undisputed center of AI innovation, but its influence extends far beyond the geographic boundaries of the San Francisco Bay Area. The region's unique ecosystem, which combines venture capital, technical talent, risk tolerance, and moonshot thinking, has created a gravitational pull that attracts AI talent and investment from around the world.

This ecosystem reflects deep American values: individual business success, market-driven innovation, and the belief that technology can solve any problem if you throw enough money and determination at it. The result is an approach to AI that focuses on creating amazing new capabilities and fast growth first, and only then worrying about government rules and effects on society.

That being said, North America's AI scene goes far beyond Silicon Valley. Toronto's Vector Institute has become a global center for AI exploration, building on Canada's tradition of government funding in scientific research, as well as the country's collaborative approach to innovation.[1] Research Triangle Park in North Carolina combines top university research with practical business applications.[2] New York's Financial District has become a cornerstone for using AI in trading, risk management, and economic decision-making.

The Cultural Context of American AI

American AI development is deeply influenced by what sociologists call "techno-optimism." It refers to the belief that technological progress is directly proportional to human progress. This shows up in AI applications that focus on connecting, sustaining, optimizing, or growing.

This cultural background creates both strengths and weaknesses. On one hand, it results in a strong drive to push industry boundaries, leading to breakthrough applications, global trendsetting, and cross-industry integration that happens at record speeds. On the other hand, this can lead to projects where innovation moves faster than governance, placing social risks and long-term sustainability on the backburner.

2.2 ASIA-PACIFIC: SPEED AND SCALE

China's Coordinated Revolution

In 2017, the Chinese government announced the ambitious New Generation AI Development Plan to become the world's leading AI innovation center by 2030.[3] This initiative is backed by massive state investment and a willingness to use AI at a societal scale.[4]

This approach builds on China's long history of combining government leadership with business competition. In this way, the government provides strategic direction and resources, while companies like Baidu, Alibaba, and Tencent execute with business drive and creativity. The result is AI implementation at a scale and speed that would be impossible to achieve in countries where individual choices take priority over collective action.

Chinese AI development is characterized by systemic integration, which refers to the belief that AI applications should be embedded into every aspect of social and economic life, rather than remaining isolated tools.[5] This has led to innovations such as super-apps that combine dozens of AI-powered services, as well as smart cities that coordinate traffic, energy, and security through integrated AI networks.

Japan's Human-Centric Approach

Japan's AI strategy is shaped by their cultural value of "wa" (harmony), and the practical dilemma of an aging population. Thus, Japanese companies build AI to make workers more effective at their jobs instead of eliminating those jobs altogether. You can see this clearly in Japan's world-leading robotics industry, where robots are designed to collaborate with people rather than take their place.

The Japanese concept of "monozukuri" (the art of making things well) influences how AI gets used in manufacturing. Instead of viewing AI as a way to eliminate human craftsmanship, Japanese companies use AI to support and protect traditional manufacturing wisdom. Toyota's production system, for example, uses AI to optimize processes while preserving the human expertise and constant improvement mindset that has made the company so successful.[6]

India's Inclusive Innovation

India's AI approach is guided by the philosophy of "vasudhaiva kutumbakam"—the world is one family. It promotes the idea that we are all responsible for each other and should thus make decisions that consider the well-being of others as well as our own. This includes using AI to address social challenges and create jobs for everyone. The government's National Strategy for Artificial Intelligence, which encompasses the idea of "AI for All," focuses on applications in healthcare, agriculture, education, and urban development that benefit the entire population, particularly in areas that are often overlooked.[7]

2.3 EUROPE: THE REGULATORY PIONEER

Brussels as the Global Rule-Maker

The European Union, headquartered in Brussels, has established itself as the world's top authority on AI rules and ethics. Its AI Act is widely regarded as the world's first comprehensive law surrounding AI. The EU's approach to AI reflects long-held European beliefs such as social democracy, individual rights, and what Germans call "technikfolgenabschätzung," which entails carefully assessing how new technology will affect people before allowing it to be widely used.[8]

European AI development focuses on building systems that are clear about how they work, can be held accountable, and respect basic human rights. This creates a different approach to building new technology compared to the United States or China, where moving fast and building powerful systems often comes before worrying about ethical issues.

Germany's Industrial Integration

Germany's approach to AI builds on the country's expertise in advanced manufacturing, as well as its cultural focus on engineering perfection. The idea of "Industry 4.0," combining AI and smart devices to create largely automated factories, originated in Germany in the early 2010s, shows a typically German outlook of handling technological change: careful, complete, and aimed at staying ahead in manufacturing.[9]

German AI development focuses on improving the country's existing industrial advantages rather than disrupting them. This has created world-class applications in motor vehicle development, factory efficiency systems, and energy management tools.

2.4 EMERGING MARKETS: LEAPFROG OPPORTUNITIES

Africa's Mobile-First Innovation

Africa's AI development follows the concept of "leapfrog innovation," which refers to the use of advanced technology to bypass older stages of development. Since most Africans use mobile phones instead of computers, the continent's mobile-first approach has created unique opportunities for AI applications that might not be as useful in more developed markets.[10]

A prime example of this is Kenya's M-Pesa mobile money system, which has become a platform for AI-powered financial services that target people who don't have access to traditional banks.[11] Solutions like these address the specific needs of their target demographic, allowing them to avoid traditional systems—in this case the banking system—that may not be beneficial to their day-to-day.

Oil Wealth Fueling Middle Eastern AI

AI development in the Middle East is driven by the region's oil wealth and its prime location for global trade. Countries like the UAE and Saudi Arabia are spending big money on AI projects. For example, Dubai is making efforts to become the world's smartest city, having jumped eight spots in the 2025 IMD Smart City Index to secure the 4th position globally.[12]

The region is now focusing on utilizing AI to rely less on oil and create new ways to make money. This appears in services such as AI-powered shipping and delivery systems that take advantage of the Middle East's location between Europe, Asia, and Africa.[13]

2.5 THE CHALLENGE OF GLOBAL POWER IMBALANCE

Despite AI's wide range of applications around the world, the core AI technologies are controlled by just a few wealthy countries and big tech companies, while billions of people have no voice in developing the systems that increasingly control their daily lives. The U.S. is widening its commanding lead in global AI investment, where private funding hit $109 billion in 2024, nearly 12 times higher than China's $9.3 billion.[14] At the same time, Africa receives just 0.02% of global AI funding,[15] a minuscule share considering Africa is home to about 18% of the global population.

This concentration of AI power creates the "digital colonialism" that many fear will inevitably happen. When advanced AI systems make decisions about loans, healthcare, and jobs for people in countries that had nothing to do with creating these technologies, that fear becomes very real. When people from marginalized communities are unable to use AI systems because they were trained on foreign data, the global power gap becomes very evident.

The problem gets worse because building AI requires huge amounts of data, computing power, and skilled workers. Countries without these resources become dependent on AI systems they can't control, understand, or change to fit their own needs and values. This creates a new type of inequality where being dependent on technology replaces older forms of economic dependence, potentially keeping developing countries from benefiting from AI while still exposing them to all its dangers.

SECTION 3: INDUSTRY AND ECONOMIC DYNAMICS

3.1 INDUSTRY-SPECIFIC ADOPTION PATTERNS

Healthcare: Where Culture Meets Regulation

The use of AI in healthcare shows how cultural beliefs, government rules, and technology skills all work together in complicated ways. In the United States, medical AI focuses heavily on efficiency and cost reduction, reflecting the market-driven nature of the American healthcare system. AI applications prioritize diagnostic speed, administrative automation, and predictive analytics that can reduce costs and wait times.

In Europe, on the other hand, patient rights and ethical concerns come first. As a result of GDPR, European healthcare AI systems must be clear about how they make decisions and give patients control over their own data. This calls for a different design of their applications when compared to systems that focus mainly on working fast and delivering efficiency.

Asian healthcare AI reflects yet another set of different cultural values, influencing beliefs surrounding how doctors and patients should interact, and whether decisions should focus on the individual or the group. Japanese AI systems are designed to enhance the doctor's authority and expertise rather than questioning or replacing medical judgment.[16] Chinese healthcare AI systems tend to focus on improving health for entire populations based on surrounding factors. They are more willing to use personal data to benefit society as a whole.[17]

Financial Services: Trust Across Cultures

AI's application in financial services shows how cultural concepts of trust, authority, and risk vary across societies. American financial AI focuses on individual empowerment and market efficiency, with applications like robo-advisors that place investment decisions into individual hands.[18]

Financial AI in Europe must navigate complex privacy regulations and cultural expectations of transparency. The "right to explainability" under GDPR means that European financial AI systems must be able to explain their decision-making processes in ways that might not be required in other jurisdictions.[19]

Asian financial AI showcases diverse cultural approaches to authority and collective responsibility. Chinese systems, for instance, readily integrate social data and government information, reflecting a comfort of using such data.[20] Similarly, Japanese financial AI prioritizes consensus-building and risk mitigation, focusing on stability rather than solely on aggressive optimization.

Manufacturing: The Automation Spectrum

AI adoption in the manufacturing sector shows different cultural attitudes toward work, automation, and human–machine collaboration. Germany focuses on precision, quality, and the preservation of skilled craftsmanship alongside automation. The concept of "intelligent manufacturing" there focuses on enhancing human capabilities rather than replacing workers.

Japan's process reflects similar values, where kaizen, along with a respect for specialized craftsmanship, are applied in order to capture and enhance traditional manufacturing wisdom rather than overtaking it entirely.

Chinese manufacturing AI prioritizes scale and efficiency, reflecting the country's role as the world's manufacturing hub. This approach emphasizes complete automation where possible and rapid adaptation to changing market demands.

3.2 THE GREAT AI ECONOMY RACE

United States: Market-Driven Dominance

The American approach to AI business development is built on core beliefs of entrepreneurship, market competition, and individual achievement. This creates a system that excels at inventing new applications and growing their businesses quickly, but also one that faces trouble with teamwork and solving problems together as a society.

American tech companies like Google, Microsoft, and Amazon have achieved global AI dominance through a combination of technical excellence, aggressive scaling, and massive capital investment. This success shows how American companies thrive through competition, but this approach also creates challenges. When AI power is concentrated just in a few large companies, it raises concerns about market power and whether regular citizens have any say in decisions. What is potentially even more troublesome is that this level of rapid development often leads to neglect of social impacts and long-term sustainability goals.

China: State-Coordinated Ambition

China's approach represents the biggest government-led AI development plan ever seen. The national AI plan combines government leadership with business execution, huge public spending with entrepreneurial drive, and long-term planning that can still adapt quickly based on market conditions.

This approach has produced remarkable results in terms of scale and speed. Chinese AI applications serve hundreds of millions of users, process vast amounts of data, and integrate across multiple sectors in ways that would be difficult to achieve in less coordinated systems.

China's method shows us that focused, large-scale initiatives can accelerate technological advancement very quickly. This model offers valuable insight into achieving rapid progress with strategic alignment in competitive fields.

European Union: The Regulatory Alternative

The European approach represents an in-between of American market-driven development and Chinese state-led coordination. The EU positions itself as the global regulator of AI, setting its own terms for sustainable AI development rather than conforming to American or Chinese standards.

This has led to global leadership in AI regulation and ethics, with the EU AI Act potentially setting international standards for the future, similar to how GDPR has influenced global privacy practices. European companies may not dominate global AI markets, but European values and regulations are increasingly shaping how AI is developed and deployed worldwide.

SECTION 4: CULTURAL AND SOCIAL DIMENSIONS

4.1 TRUST AND PRIVACY: INDIVIDUAL VS. COLLECTIVE VALUES

How countries develop and deploy AI is directly impacted by their different cultural values, especially when it comes to data privacy. Western societies often focus strongly on individual rights, which leads to data protection laws such as GDPR and the California Consumer Privacy Act (CCPA). Other cultures prioritize collective benefits, leading to very different AI approaches.

Meanwhile, many Asian societies, especially those shaped by Confucian values such as social responsibility, are more willing to accept some privacy tradeoffs to improve collective security and efficiency. This contrast is the reason why the development of AI in these regions focuses more on public benefit and social governance.

The concept of ubuntu, or compassion, from South African philosophy, offers us another perspective on this balance. Ubuntu suggests that individual well-being and collective well-being are inseparable. This view introduces the option of making AI applications that serve both individual and community needs simultaneously.

4.2 WORK AND DIGNITY ACROSS CULTURES

Different cultures have contrasting views surrounding work, automation, and respect. These differences greatly affect how they adopt AI. For example, the Protestant work ethic that shapes many Western countries focuses on individual success through hard work, which can make people resistant to AI, which they see as a threat taking away meaningful jobs.

East Asian societies, influenced by concepts such as the Japanese "ikigai" (life purpose) and the Chinese emphasis on collective progress, approach AI automation differently. These cultures are more willing to accept job displacement if it contributes to overall social advancement, but they also emphasize the importance of finding new forms of meaningful contribution.

4.3 SOCIAL CONTRACT AND AI GOVERNANCE

Different countries have different ideas about how citizens, governments, and tech companies should work together to manage AI. These cultural differences create completely different approaches to AI rules and oversight.

Scandinavian societies, where trust is strong and the government is open about what it does, are comfortable letting the government lead AI regulation and run public AI programs. Citizens trust that government AI systems will be used properly and that people will have a democratic say in AI policies.

American society, with its cultural focus on limiting government power and protecting individual rights, prefers market-driven AI development with minimal government interference. This creates resistance to large-scale AI regulation and a preference for industry self-regulation.

Chinese society, shaped by its history of strong central governance and a focus on collective progress, readily accepts heavy government involvement in AI development and use. This framework makes it easy to have highly coordinated national AI strategies, allowing for rapid advancement and large-scale implementation of technological projects.

SECTION 5: THE FUTURE OF AI REGULATION—GLOBAL IMPACT

5.1 REGULATORY CONVERGENCE VS. DIVERGENCE

One of the most critical questions facing global AI development is whether regulations will converge toward common standards or continue to diverge along cultural and political lines. The answer will determine the future of global business, international cooperation, and technological development.

There are several good reasons why countries might end up with similar AI rules. AI technologies are global in nature: algorithms developed in one country are deployed worldwide, data flows across borders, and AI systems often require international cooperation to function effectively. Global challenges like climate change, pandemic response, and economic inequality all require coordinated AI approaches that go beyond national boundaries.

The European Union's AI Act represents the most ambitious attempt we've seen so far to create regulatory frameworks that could become global standards. Just like Europe's GDPR, which greatly impacted global data and privacy practices, the AI Act could create what scholars call the "Brussels Effect," where European regulations become global norms because companies find it easier to adopt common standards than to maintain separate compliance systems for different markets.

Even so, the forces that pull countries apart are just as powerful. Different societies have fundamentally different beliefs about privacy, government authority, individual rights, and responsibility to the community. These differences reflect deep cultural and philosophical traditions that cannot easily be merged through international agreements.

5.2 CROSS-BORDER AI GOVERNANCE CHALLENGES

The global nature of AI creates new challenges we have never faced before, especially for the traditional governance systems based on national sovereignty and territorial boundaries. When an AI system trained in one country uses data from multiple nations and makes decisions that affect people in yet another country, which jurisdiction's laws apply?

Data localization requirements illustrate this complexity. These days, many countries require certain types of data to be stored and processed within national boundaries. But AI systems often require access to global datasets to function effectively. Companies must navigate a complex web of conflicting requirements that can make global AI deployment expensive or even impossible.

Intellectual property and technology transfer disputes add another layer of complexity. The United States has placed export regulations on AI chips and software to China. At the same time, China has developed domestic alternatives to reduce dependence on American technology. These technological decoupling efforts create parallel AI ecosystems that become increasingly incompatible over time.[21]

5.3 BUSINESS STRATEGY IMPLICATIONS: NAVIGATING COMPLEXITY

Regulatory complexity creates both problems and opportunities, especially for companies that work around the world. They must develop something called "regulatory intelligence," which refers to the ability to monitor, understand, and adjust to changing regulatory environments across multiple jurisdictions. For instance, legal teams must understand not only current regulations but also emerging regulatory trends. Product development teams must design systems that can adapt to different country requirements without losing core features. Business strategy teams must consider regulatory risk when deciding which market to enter and expand into.

Some companies are responding by adopting a "regulatory arbitrage" strategy—that is, to relocate AI development and deployment to jurisdictions with favorable regulatory environments. However, this approach has its limitations, particularly as governments become more sophisticated about preventing regulatory shopping.

More sophisticated companies are adopting what could be called "regulatory resilience" strategies: building AI systems that can adapt to multiple regulatory frameworks and even anticipate future regulatory changes. Although this will require higher upfront investment, it creates more sustainable competitive advantages in the long run.

5.4 INTERNATIONAL COOPERATION EFFORTS

Regulatory divergence is causing many challenges in global businesses. However, major efforts are being made to create international cooperation frameworks for AI governance. The G7 and G20 have established working groups on AI governance, the United Nations has created an advisory body for AI regulation,[22] and industry organizations are developing voluntary standards that could become the basis for government regulations.

These efforts reflect a growing recognition that some AI challenges, particularly those related to safety, security, and global risks, require international cooperation regardless of cultural and political differences. Climate modeling AI, pandemic response systems, and nuclear safety applications all require global coordination to be effective.

The OECD AI Principles, adopted in 2019, show one successful example of international cooperation on AI governance. These principles have influenced national AI strategies and regulatory systems around the world, despite the fact that they aren't legally binding.[23] This proves that countries are able to find agreement on even the most complicated and culturally sensitive international issues.

5.5 INDUSTRY SELF-REGULATION VS. GOVERNMENT OVERSIGHT

Regions take drastically different approaches when it comes to regulating technology development. Some tend to leave the industry to self-regulate, while others rely on governments to provide the oversight.

Silicon Valley has traditionally followed a "move fast and break things" philosophy, prioritizing rapid innovation and market-driven solutions. Under this approach, companies launch products very quickly, test them in real-world conditions, and address problems as they arise. This strategy helps breakthrough technologies reach consumers faster, but it sometimes creates issues that require government intervention after problems have already emerged.

European regulators believe in safety first. They prefer to establish comprehensive laws and oversight mechanisms first, before new technologies are widely adopted by the public. This approach can make innovation slower, but it benefits the business by making the rules clear from the start.

The most effective regulatory frameworks combine the strengths from both models. In this merged model, industry leaders bring essential technical expertise, underlining what is practically achievable using emerging technologies, while government oversight provides democratic accountability and ensures that public interests are protected alongside private innovation.

The key challenge is designing systems that take full advantage of industry knowledge, while maintaining meaningful public oversight and democratic participation in decisions that affect society as a whole.

SECTION 6: STRATEGIC IMPLEMENTATION AND FUTURE OUTLOOK

6.1 MARKET ENTRY CONSIDERATIONS: BEYOND TECHNICAL FEASIBILITY

For businesses considering global AI deployment, technical feasibility is only the starting point for strategic analysis. Cultural adaptation requirements may be even more important than regulatory compliance in determining success or failure in specific markets.

Consider the case of an American AI company developing sophisticated chatbot technology for customer service. In English-speaking markets, customers are comfortable with direct, efficient interactions. But when deployed in Japan, customer satisfaction scores were poor, because Japanese customers are used to more formal, contextual interactions that show appropriate respect for social hierarchy (e.g. addressing the client properly).

The solution requires cultural intelligence, in addition to language translation. Successful deployment will have redesigns in which conversation flows according to Japanese communication patterns and AI systems are trained on culturally appropriate responses. Customer relationship management is effectively combined with local business practice norms.

Similarly, AI systems designed for individual users may not work well in cultures where decisions are made by groups. For instance, in parts of East Asia, streaming services would have to suggest content suitable for multiple viewers, as watching TV is typically a group activity.

6.2 GLOBAL AI SUPPLY CHAIN MANAGEMENT

Managing AI development across global supply chains requires new approaches to talent sourcing, data governance, and technology integration. The traditional model of centralized AI development doesn't work well when different markets require unique approaches to privacy, regulation, and cultural adaptation.

Leading companies are developing distributed AI development models, in which foundations are built in multiple regions to exchange knowledge and resources among each other.[24] This requires new forms of cross-cultural collaboration and knowledge management.

Data governance becomes particularly complex in global AI supply chains. Different jurisdictions have different requirements for data localization, privacy protection, and cross-border data transfers. Companies must develop data architecture that can support AI development while complying with multiple, sometimes conflicting, legal requirements.

6.3 COMPETITIVE INTELLIGENCE AND POSITIONING

To understand the global AI race, it is important to look beyond just technology. Government policies, cultural values, and strategic goals are just as important in shaping how AI develops around the world.

For example, Chinese AI firms have strong government backing and vast amounts of data, but their global expansion is often limited by geopolitical tensions. European AI companies are leaders in privacy and ethical innovation, although they sometimes lack the scale of larger markets. American tech giants may have a widespread international presence but are dealing with growing regulation and cultural pushback. A successful global AI strategy means recognizing these differences and using them to your company's advantage.

6.4 POTENTIAL GLOBAL AI EVOLUTION

Looking ahead, the global AI landscape will likely take one of three distinct paths, each with significant impacts on businesses, governments, and society as a whole.

Scenario 1: Global Alignment and Cooperation

In this instance, the world comes together to create shared laws for AI. This is likely to be triggered by a major global event, such as a serious AI safety failure or a worldwide crisis that requires a coordinated AI response.

The result is the establishment of international AI standards, similar to those for aviation or for the internet. While nations can modify these rules on a local level, the core principles become universal. This environment is ideal for companies that operate on a global scale, making it easier for the world to tackle far-reaching problems together.

Scenario 2: A Divided World of AI Nationalism

In this future, global differences in politics and culture prevent any real cooperation. Instead, major world regions each build their own AI systems based on their own rules, standards, and values.

This results in a fractured global landscape. This scenario is often called the "Balkanization" of AI, in which these separate AI ecosystems have trouble connecting. For businesses, this means they cannot have a single global strategy. Instead, they must tailor their approach to suit each region. Companies in this scenario will have to deal with increased cost and complexity of operations, but it will also create immense opportunities for those that can adapt to different markets.

Scenario 3: Emerging Markets Leap Ahead

This future provides the opportunity for some countries, especially those with fast-growing economies, to become unexpected AI leaders. If we look at countries like India, Nigeria, or Brazil, they have vast and young populations, widespread mobile phone use, and flexible regulatory environments. These are favorable conditions for pioneering new kinds of AI applications. Developed countries might adopt these innovations after seeing their initial success.

This technological leapfrogging is becoming increasingly popular, where regions skip outdated technologies and jump directly to advanced solutions. In AI, this could mean that certain markets develop more practical, affordable, or socially conscious AI tools that eventually set new standards for the rest of the world.

6.5 PREPARING FOR AN UNCERTAIN AI FUTURE

Certain capabilities will be absolutely essential for navigating the global AI landscape successfully, regardless of which scenario emerges. These include cultural intelligence that enables effective operation across different cultural contexts, regulatory agility that allows adaptation to changing governance frameworks, and ethical reasoning that guides responsible AI development across different value systems.

The most successful organizations will be those that are able to build adaptive global AI strategies with approaches that remain effective regardless of how the global landscape evolves. This requires investing in cross-cultural competency, maintaining flexibility in technology architectures, and developing a deep understanding of the cultural and political forces shaping AI development worldwide.

6.6 THE PATH FORWARD: INTEGRATING GLOBAL WISDOM

The future of AI will more likely than not be shaped by the dynamic interplay of different cultures, regulations, and innovation styles around the world, rather than that of one country or one school of thought.

A helpful way to look at this is through the Chinese idea of "Da Tong" (大同), literally meaning "unity through diversity." True global leadership in AI will come from blending the best ideas from different traditions into one.

Silicon Valley's entrepreneurial energy, China's coordinated ambition, Europe's ethical leadership, India's inclusive innovation, the Middle East's well-resourced initiatives, and Africa's leapfrog creativity all contribute essential perspectives to global AI development. The leaders and organizations that are able to synthesize these different approaches, including those that can think like entrepreneurs while considering ethical implications and can move quickly while building social consensus, will be best-positioned for success in the global AI economy.

This requires seeing both the forest and the trees—or in this case, seeing both the universal principles and local variations, that shape how AI is being developed and deployed around the world. Like the Silk Road, which connected different civilizations while allowing each to maintain its unique characteristics, the global AI ecosystem will thrive through both connection and diversity.

Moving forward requires humility, curiosity, and a shared commitment to ensure AI benefits all of humanity. By learning from each other, we can create a future that values both innovation and ethics, efficiency and empathy, individual success and the common good.

As the great Indian philosopher Rabindranath Tagore once wrote, "the butterfly counts not months but moments, and has time enough." In this fast-moving world of AI, we must learn to balance this sense of urgency with the patience required to build inclusive, fair, and sustainable AI for a better world and a better future.

NOTES

1. "News release: New Artificial Intelligence Research Institute Launched in Toronto." *Vector Institute*, 2017, vectorinstitute.ai/press-release-new-artificial-intelligence-research-institute-launched-in-toronto/.
2. "Research Triangle Park: A Model for University Research and Economic Growth." *Public Ed Works*, 2014, publicedworks.org/2014/10/research-triangle-park-a-model-for-university-research-and-economic-growth/.
3. Karch, Theodore J., et al. "China's Vision for The Next Generation of Artificial Intelligence." *The National Law Review*, 2018, natlawreview.com/article/china-s-vision-next-generation-artificial-intelligence.
4. Moss, Sebastian. "China Announces Major AI Plans, Hopes to Become World Leader by 2030." *Data Center Dynamics*, 2017, datacenterdynamics.com/en/news/china-announces-major-ai-plans-hopes-to-become-world-leader-by-2030/.
5. Webster, Graham, et al. "Full Translation: China's 'New Generation Artificial Intelligence Development Plan'." *New America*, 2017, newamerica.org/cybersecurity-initiative/digichina/blog/full-translation-chinas-new-generation-artificial-intelligence-development-plan-2017/.
6. Chen, May Yee. "Toyota Is Deploying AI Agents to Harness the Collective Wisdom of Engineers and Innovate Faster." *Microsoft Source*, 2024, news.microsoft.com/source/asia/features/toyota-is-deploying-ai-agents-to-harness-the-collective-wisdom-of-engineers-and-innovate-faster.
7. *Responsible AI*. NITI Aayog, 2021, niti.gov.in/sites/default/files/2021-02/Responsible-AI-22022021.pdf.
8. "Understanding the EU AI Act: Requirements and Next Steps." *ISACA*, 2024, isaca.org/resources/white-papers/2024/understanding-the-eu-ai-act.
9. Winter, Jeff. "Industry 4.0 and Smart Manufacturing." *International Society of Automation*, 2022, isa.org/intech-home/2022/august-2022/features/introduction-the-birth-of-industry-4-0-and-smart-m.
10. Ramanathan, Srikumar. "The Role Of Leapfrog Innovation In Emerging Markets." *Forbes*, 2023, forbes.com/councils/forbestechcouncil/2023/05/31/the-role-of-leapfrog-innovation-in-emerging-markets/.
11. Conduit, "What is M-Pesa? A Revolutionary Change in Africa's Digital Economy." *Conduit Financial*, 2025, conduitpay.com/blog/what-is-m-pesa-a-revolutionary-change-in-africas-digital-economy.
12. "Dubai Ranks 4th Globally in IMD Smart City Index 2025." *Government of Dubai Media Office*, 2025, mediaoffice.ae/en/news/2025/may/12-05/dubai-ranks-4th-globally-in-imd-smart-city-index-2025.
13. "AI for Logistics: Tracking, Scheduling & Automation." *Arabot*, arabot.io/en/industries/logistics.

14. "The 2025 AI Index Report." *Stanford Institute for Human-Centered AI*, 2025, hai.stanford.edu/ai-index/2025-ai-index-report.
15. Ashiru, Grace. "Africa Receives Just 0.02% of Global AI Funding in Q2 2025 Amid $47.3 Billion Surge." *Tech in Africa*, 2025, techinafrica.com/africa-receives-just-0-02-of-global-ai-funding-in-q2-2025-amid-47-3-billion-surge/.
16. Tochibayashi, Naoako. Kutty, Naoko. "Three AI Tools Revolutionising Healthcare in Japan." *World Economic Forum*, 2023, weforum.org/stories/2023/12/three-ai-tools-setting-the-stage-for-a-tech-revolution-by-japans-entrepreneurial-doctors/.
17. Simonite, Tom. "Chinese Hospitals Deploy AI to Help Diagnose Covid-19." *Wired*, 2020, wired.com/story/chinese-hospitals-deploy-ai-help-diagnose-covid-19/.
18. Hall, Jessica. "Most Workers Still Struggle to Invest in Their Retirement. This Could Help." *MarketWatch*, 2024, marketwatch.com/story/most-workers-still-struggle-to-invest-in-their-retirement-heres-how-cheap-robo-advisers-can-help-c5fc23f7.
19. Marquet, Enzo. "CJEU Confirms the 'Right to Explainability' in Automated Decision-Making: What It Means for Your Business." *Cranium*, 2025, cranium.eu/right-to-explainability/.
20. Wei, He. "Zhima Credit Makes Visa Applications Easier." *China Daily*, 2018, global.chinadaily.com.cn/a/201811/27/WS5bfc7b8da310eff30328b256.html.
21. Barczentewicz, Mikołaj. "US Export Controls on AI and Semiconductors." *International Center for Law and Economics*, 2025, laweconcenter.org/resources/us-export-controls-on-ai-and-semiconductors/.
22. Agence France-Presse. "UN Creates Artificial Intelligence Advisory Panel." *CTV News*, 2025, ctvnews.ca/sci-tech/article/un-creates-artificial-intelligence-advisory-panel/.
23. "AI Principles." *Organisation for Economic Co-operation and Development*, 2024, oecd.org/en/topics/ai-principles.html.
24. "NVIDIA Partners With Europe Model Builders and Cloud Providers to Accelerate Region's Leap Into AI." *NVIDIA Newsroom*, 2025, nvidianews.nvidia.com/news/nvidia-partners-with-europe-model-builders-and-cloud-providers-to-accelerate-regions-leap-into-ai.

CHAPTER 9

The Future of AI in Business

Navigating Uncertainty and Opportunity

STANDING AT THE INFLECTION POINT

I've spent the last two decades watching technology waves reshape entire industries, but nothing has felt quite like this moment. What we are living through may be the most profound breakthrough in human history.

The artificial intelligence (AI) revolution is moving at unprecedented speeds. Just five years ago, the idea of having a conversation with an AI bot that could help you write code, analyze complex data, or brainstorm creative solutions seemed like science fiction. Today, millions of professionals start their day by collaborating with AI systems. They have become an integral part of people's workflow, similar to email or spreadsheets.

I've talked to CEOs who have gone from AI skeptics to true believers in the span of six months, not because someone sold them on the technology, but because they saw their competitors gaining ground they couldn't explain. Stories like this remind me that while the technology is remarkable, the human element, how we choose to integrate AI into our lives, ultimately determines whether this transformation creates value or chaos.

The framework I want to share with you isn't about predicting exactly which AI breakthrough will emerge next or when your industry will reach

DOI: 10.1201/9781003644699-9

peak automation. Instead, it's about building the organizational capacity to thrive in uncertainty, rather than just survive in it.

Here is what I've learned from watching hundreds of organizations navigate this transition: the companies that emerge stronger aren't necessarily the ones with the most advanced AI implementations. They are the ones that figured out how to learn alongside their systems, constantly adapting their strategies, cultures, and capabilities as the AI landscape evolves.

This requires three fundamental mindset shifts that I've seen work across several industries. First, we need to stop planning for specific technologies and start building the capacity for technological change itself. That particular AI tool you deploy today will likely be obsolete in two years, but your organization's ability to evaluate, adopt, and integrate new technologies will remain infinitely valuable.

Second, we must evolve from viewing AI as a sophisticated tool to understanding it as a collaborative partner. As stressed constantly throughout this book, the most successful AI implementations I have encountered don't replace human judgment but amplify it instead. They don't eliminate the need for creativity, empathy, and strategic thinking. Instead, they create more space for those uniquely human capabilities to flourish.

Third, we need to transition from reactive responses to proactive preparation for AI's broader implications. The organizations that thrive won't just be the ones that implement AI well. They will be the ones that help shape how AI evolves in ways that benefit their stakeholders and society as a whole.

SECTION 1: AI'S NEXT FRONTIER

1.1 BEYOND CURRENT CAPABILITIES: EMERGING AI TECHNOLOGIES

Let me paint a picture of where we are heading, based on conversations I've had with researchers, entrepreneurs, and early adopters who are building tomorrow's AI applications today.

Multimodal AI systems represent perhaps the most exciting frontier that I am tracking. Imagine walking into a retail store where the AI assistant doesn't just respond to your spoken questions, it simultaneously processes your facial expressions, analyzes your clothing style, considers the weather outside, and remembers your purchase history to provide recommendations that feel almost telepathic in their relevance.

These systems will fundamentally change how we analyze and understand complex business problems. Marketing teams will soon analyze not just what customers say in surveys, but how they say it, what they're looking at, and how their behavior changes across different contexts; manufacturing operations will integrate visual quality control with acoustic monitoring and performance data to predict equipment failures with uncanny accuracy.

Autonomous agents represent another transformation that feels both inevitable and slightly unsettling. Unlike today's AI assistants that respond to specific requests, these agents pursue complex objectives independently. Early versions are already managing entire customer service cases from initial contact through resolution, coordinating with multiple departments and following up weeks later to ensure satisfaction.[1]

What's happening to the field of knowledge work is profound. In legal firms, autonomous agents now handle initial case research, identifying relevant precedents and drafting preliminary analyses that used to take junior associates weeks to complete. Attorneys have by no means been replaced, but rather, they have been elevated to focus on strategy, client relationships, and complex argumentation that requires human judgment and creativity.[2]

1.2 THE EVOLUTION OF AUTOMATION

The journey from basic to intelligent automation is fascinating to witness firsthand. If we look at traditional automation, it involves having reliable machinery that follows instructions perfectly but can't handle anything outside of what it was originally designed to do. Intelligent automation is like having a robot colleague who can think through problems, adapt to new situations, and actually improve alongside you over time.

I remember my visit to a financial services company two years ago. At the time, their loan applications were processed through rigid formula-based systems. Customers with unusual but legitimate financial situations were automatically rejected, leading to lost business and frustrated applicants. Today, their AI-powered system analyzes hundreds of data points, considers context and nuance, and makes decisions that are both more accurate and more fair than their old system was capable of.

But here is what I find most encouraging about this automation revolution: it's revealing what makes us uniquely human. As AI handles more routine analysis and decision-making, the premium on creativity, emotional intelligence, and complex relationship management has actually increased. The best performers in AI-augmented organizations will be those who can collaborate effectively with AI systems while bringing distinctly human insights to the table.

1.3 REDEFINING HUMAN–AI COLLABORATION

Observing organizations that get human–AI collaboration right have taught me less about the technology and more about the relationship dynamic itself. The most successful partnerships I've encountered feel less like human-vs.-machine and more like expert-consulting-with-expert.

I spent time with a journalism team that has figured out how to use AI for data analysis and generating initial drafts; but their success lies in their efforts to preserve the human elements that make their reporting compelling. AI processes vast amounts of information and identifies patterns that would take their team of reporters weeks to uncover. That being said, humans are better at conducting interviews, providing context, and crafting stories that connect with readers emotionally. The result is journalism that is both more comprehensive and more engaging than either humans or AI could produce alone.

The psychology of these partnerships is crucial. I have noticed that teams with the most effective human–AI collaboration have developed what I call "appropriate trust." They understand what AI does well and where it falls short. They have developed the ability to challenge AI recommendations when their own experience reveals potential problems, while also being open to insights that contradict their initial assumptions.

Building this trust requires transparency. The most successful implementations I have seen involve AI systems that can explain their decisions in plain language. Successful teams will always want to understand the data and logic behind AI's recommendations. This transparency builds team confidence and helps them identify when AI might be missing important context.

1.4 ORGANIZATIONAL STRUCTURES IN THE AI ERA

The organizational charts of AI-native companies look different from traditional hierarchies, and for good reason. When AI systems can process information and make routine decisions automatically, many traditional management layers become bottlenecks rather than value-adding functions.

The most successful AI-integrated organizations tend to be flatter, with managers focusing on strategic thinking, team development, and complex problem-solving rather than the processing of information and routine decision approval. An example of this is reducing the number of management layers within a company, which improves decision speed and quality through streamlined communication channels and more efficient feedback loops.

New roles are emerging that didn't exist five years ago. AI trainers now work to help systems understand business context and desired outcomes.[3] There are also AI interpreters, who help teams understand complex AI recommendations and translate between technical capabilities and business needs.[4] These roles require a unique combination of technical understanding, business acumen, and communication skills that traditional job categories don't capture.

SECTION 2: PREPARING FOR AI'S IMPACT ON PRIVACY, SECURITY, AND EMPLOYMENT

2.1 PRIVACY IN AN AI-DRIVEN WORLD

The privacy challenges we are facing with AI go far beyond traditional data protection concerns. I have had countless conversations with business leaders who are grappling with questions that didn't exist just a few years ago. For example, when AI analyzes customer behavior to provide personalized services, who owns the insights generated? How do we balance the incredible value of AI-powered personalization with respect for individual privacy?

The unpredictability of AI insights creates unique challenges. A customer's purchase history might reveal health conditions, financial stress, or relationship changes that they never intended to share. While this capability could drive valuable personalized marketing, it also raises profound questions surrounding consent and privacy boundaries.

Privacy-preserving AI techniques offer hope for resolving these tensions. Federated learning, for example, allows AI systems to learn from distributed data without centralizing sensitive information. I have seen healthcare applications where hospitals can collaboratively train AI diagnostic systems without sharing patient data, achieving better outcomes while maintaining privacy protection.

It is becoming very challenging for organizations operating across jurisdictions, as the regulatory landscape is evolving very rapidly. I regularly advise companies on how to navigate different privacy requirements such as GDPR, CCPA, and emerging AI-specific regulations. The organizations I have seen handling this challenge best are those adopting privacy-by-design approaches. These systems build protection into AI systems instead of treating it as a compliance afterthought.

2.2 SECURITY CHALLENGES AND SOLUTIONS

The cybersecurity landscape has become dramatically more complex with AI adoption. Sophisticated attacks are manipulating AI systems by providing carefully crafted inputs that cause incorrect outputs while appearing completely normal on the surface. These adversarial attacks are particularly dangerous because they can operate undetected for extended periods of time.[5]

Deepfake technology presents new risks that many organizations aren't prepared for. It's possible for companies to receive convincing audio recordings of their CEO authorizing large financial transfers. Verification procedures can detect fraud, but many organizations remain vulnerable to these AI-assisted deception attacks.

The arms race between AI security and AI-enabled threats creates ongoing challenges that require never-ending adaptation. As security systems become more sophisticated, attackers develop new techniques to bypass them. This evolutionary pressure means that AI security can never be a "set-it-and-forget-it" solution; it requires ongoing investment and attention.

2.3 THE EMPLOYMENT TRANSFORMATION

The discussions I have about AI's effect on jobs are often emotionally charged, and for good reason. Our work is so closely tied to our livelihood and our identity that the fear of being replaced by technology creates significant anxiety.

However, my experience from hundreds of AI rollouts has shown that the effect on jobs is a choice and is not predetermined as many believe. Organizations that treat AI as a way to reduce expenses often use it to replace staff. On the other hand, those that use AI to strengthen their existing capabilities tend to *invest* in their workforce. They use technology to empower people rather than replace them.

Both of the aforementioned approaches are being applied in practice, for better or for worse. For example, one manufacturing company uses AI to automate quality inspections, cutting costs in the short term.

However, they also lose the valuable insight and problem-solving skills of their experienced inspectors. Concurrently, another company uses AI to support their inspectors, enabling them to detect issues more quickly and accurately. This approach improves both product quality and employee satisfaction.

Jobs that involve routine, predictable work are often seen as the most vulnerable to automation. But even in these roles, using AI to assist people usually delivers better results than outright replacement. I worked with a financial services company that chose to use AI for initial loan screening, which freed up their loan officers to handle more complex cases and build stronger client relationships. This led to increased customer satisfaction, personalization, and better loan performance.

Preparing workers for these changes is critical. The most effective programs combine technical training with uniquely human skills, skills like creative problem-solving, emotional intelligence, and complex communication. As AI takes over an increasing amount of routine tasks, these skills become increasingly valuable.

2.4 ETHICAL AI AND RESPONSIBLE INNOVATION

We dedicated an entire chapter (Chapter 6) to the ethical challenges of AI implementation, which have become increasingly urgent as these systems gain influence over business decisions and individual lives.

Ethical AI use is becoming increasingly compelling. What used to be a choice concerning morality is becoming a powerful business strategy. Companies that prioritize responsible AI practices often gain strong customer loyalty, are more attractive to skilled employees, and can more easily comply with new regulations.

Rather than limiting innovation, ethical guidelines provide a foundation for building trust and creating a lasting competitive advantage.

SECTION 3: STRATEGIC FOUNDATIONS FOR AI PREPAREDNESS

3.1 UNDERSTANDING AI'S COMPETITIVE LANDSCAPE

The race to adopt AI is fundamentally different from past technology revolutions. Long-standing advantages such as physical infrastructure, sales networks, and proprietary information are now being disrupted by AI systems that can learn, adapt, and grow at incredible speeds.

Data is often called the new oil, but it operates very differently; its value can be created or destroyed rapidly. I have seen large companies with massive datasets fail to capitalize on them, while smaller players with smarter data strategies gain significant advantages. The key isn't just having data, it's having the right data, and the organizational capability to extract insights and act on them.

AI creates powerful network effects that redefine competition. Amazon and other platform businesses are using AI to connect user groups, such as linking buyers and sellers. They often benefit from positively reinforced cycles: the more people use their platform, the more valuable it becomes for everyone. I have also seen cases where AI promotes collaboration across entire industries, helping multiple companies succeed together rather than creating a single dominant winner. Pharmaceutical consortium MELLODDY follows this same principle, training individual machine learning models collaboratively to improve data quality and drive breakthroughs in the industry.[6]

3.2 BUILDING AI-READY ORGANIZATIONAL CULTURE

Culture eats strategy for breakfast, as Peter Drucker famously said.[7] This is especially true for AI transformation. A number of technically sound AI implementations fail because of cultural resistance, while modest AI applications are able to succeed because they are supported by cultures that embrace learning and adaptation.

AI-ready leaders think differently about control, predictability, and decision-making. They are comfortable with uncertainty and experimentation, viewing failures as learning opportunities rather than problems to be avoided. This requires a fundamental shift for leaders who built their careers on minimizing risk and maximizing predictability.

The organizations with the most successful AI cultures have created environments where teams can experiment, learn from failures, and iterate rapidly. Some see this as an unnecessary opportunity for risks, but it's really all about building structured learning processes that gain value from both what works, and what doesn't.

Psychological safety is another crucial factor for successful AI adoption. Employees must feel secure enough to challenge AI recommendations, report system errors, and test new ideas. Companies that penalize mistakes or failed experiments will discourage the very innovation needed to develop transformative AI applications.

3.3 INFRASTRUCTURE AND DATA STRATEGY CONSIDERATIONS

A strong technical foundation for AI must look beyond today's needs. Many organizations struggle because they build systems purely meant for current AI applications without planning for how quickly the technology will change.

The choice between cloud and edge computing is a strategic business decision, not just a technical one. The cloud offers scalability and advanced tools, while edge computing supports real-time processing and greater data privacy. The most successful strategies often blend elements of both, in a hybrid approach.

Data governance becomes a lot more complex with AI, as these systems often require access to diverse data sources across organizational boundaries. Effective frameworks set clear, flexible policies that emphasize data quality, security, and compliance, without stifling innovation.

Last, interoperability and vendor independence are crucial considerations that many organizations overlook in their enthusiasm to implement AI solutions. Building AI capabilities around proprietary platforms may provide short-term advantages but can also create long-term constraints as technologies and market conditions evolve. Organizations that prioritize flexibility today will be far better positioned to adapt to tomorrow's rapidly shifting AI landscape.

SECTION 4: NAVIGATING THE AI TRANSFORMATION

As I reflect on the hundreds of conversations I have had with business leaders, technologists, and employees during this age of AI transformation, I am continually reminded of two things: the tremendous opportunities that lie ahead, and the irreplaceable role that people play in making them successful.

Success isn't necessarily determined by who has the most sophisticated AI implementations or the largest technology budgets. Rather, it's based on who is able to learn and advance alongside their systems, continuously adapting their strategies, cultures, and capabilities as the AI landscape evolves.

4.1 TIMELESS WISDOM FOR MODERN CHALLENGES

In my experience working on AI projects across different organizations and countries, I've discovered that traditional wisdom often provides valuable guidance for today's technology challenges. These time-tested ideas offer practical approaches to managing rapid change, helping people adapt, and maintaining ethical leadership.

For example, Buddhist teachings on "anicca" (impermanence) and "pratītyasamutpāda" (interdependence) remind us that change is inevitable and that all things are connected. This perspective is very helpful in easing the anxiety that comes with technological disruption. I have watched leaders reshape their AI strategies after embracing this simple but powerful concept. Rather than pursuing perfect, unchanging solutions, they now prioritize building flexible systems that can adjust as needs and technologies evolve. This shift ultimately creates stronger, more resilient organizations.

In Hinduism, concepts from the Bhagavad Gita, particularly "dharma" (righteous duty), teach us to focus on our obligations regardless of the outcome. This is valuable guidance for leaders during AI transformation; it shows that we make better decisions surrounding AI development and deployment when we focus on ethical action and long-term value creation instead of short-term gains.

4.2 INTEGRATING ANCIENT WISDOM WITH MODERN STRATEGY

These philosophical traditions teach us the importance of balance, the value of patience and persistence, the necessity of ethical considerations, and the recognition that true wisdom comes from understanding interconnectedness rather than pursuing individual advantage.

The journey ahead requires us to welcome the uncertainty, treating it as a competitive advantage instead of as a problem to be solved. While we can't predict exactly which AI technologies will emerge or how quickly they will be adopted, we can build organizational capabilities that thrive in uncertain environments through experimentation, learning, and adaptation. These are the principles that echo the ancient principle of finding strength through flexibility.

The most successful AI transformations are those that are able to balance technological capabilities with human values, creating systems that enhance rather than replace human potential. These organizations recognize that AI's greatest value comes from the creative partnerships that are formed between human intelligence and AI, automation is just a bonus.

The choices we make today regarding how to develop, deploy, and govern AI systems will shape the business landscape for decades to come. If we choose approaches that focus on collaboration, ethical innovation, and continuous learning, we can create an AI-powered future that creates value for businesses, employees, and society on the whole.

Transformation is already happening whether we like it or not. The question is whether we can shape that transformation in ways that reflect our deepest values and aspirations. The organizations that get this right will be able to take advantage of the latest technology, combining it with the enduring wisdom that has guided humanity through changes for millennia.

NOTES

1. "What Are Autonomous Agents? A Complete Guide." *Salesforce*, 2025, salesforce.com/agentforce/ai-agents/autonomous-agents/.
2. McCarthy, Madi. "Is Artificial Intelligence the New Junior Lawyer?" *Association of Corporate Counsel*, 2025, acc.com/artificial-intelligence-new-junior-lawyer.
3. Faggella, Dan. "Seven Non-Technical Enterprise AI Career Paths." *Emerj*, 2022, emerj.com/seven-non-technical-ai-career-paths/.
4. Watkins, Steven. "AI Job Roles 2025: Transforming Workforce Dynamics." *Daily Cup of AI*, 2025, dailycupofai.com/blog/ai-powered-job-roles-of-2025-190/.
5. Sibanda, Isla. "The Rise of Adversarial AI in Cybersecurity: A Hidden Threat." *SecurityInfoWatch*, 2025, securityinfowatch.com/cybersecurity/article/55290072/the-rise-of-adversarial-ai-in-cybersecurity-a-hidden-threat.
6. Gautam, Akash. "MELLODDY: Turning Pharma Competition into "Coopetition"." *Kubermatic*, 2025, kubermatic.com/blog/melloddy-turning-pharma-competition-into-coopetition/.
7. Duffy, David W. "What Does Culture Eats Strategy for Breakfast Mean?" *Corporate Governance Institute*, 2025, thecorporategovernanceinstitute.com/insights/lexicon/what-does-culture-eats-strategy-for-breakfast-mean/.

CHAPTER 10

Choosing Your AI Journey

A Roadmap for Organizations and Individuals Alike

Crafting an effective artificial intelligence (AI) strategy is like trying to map a river while standing in it. The current keeps shifting, new tributaries form overnight, and water level rises unpredictably. But here's the thing: you can't wait for the river to stop flowing before you decide which way to swim.

Every week, I talk to executives who are paralyzed by the scope of AI transformation. They know they need to act, but they're overwhelmed by their options, terrified of making expensive mistakes. Meanwhile, their employees are quietly experimenting with ChatGPT, their competitors are announcing AI initiatives, and their customers are beginning to expect AI-powered experiences.

This chapter isn't going to give you a magic formula, as there isn't one. Instead, it will provide you with a framework to help assess where you are, identify where you need to go, and help you take your first steps with confidence. Whether you are leading a healthcare startup or a century-old manufacturing firm, and regardless of whether you are a CEO or a mid-level manager, the fundamentals remain the same: begin with clarity, focus on what truly matters, and commit to continuous learning.

DOI: 10.1201/9781003644699-10

But before we dive into roadmaps and frameworks, let's briefly revisit the reason why most organizations struggle with AI. It's not because the technology doesn't work; most of the time, it's because they approach AI like any other IT project. They buy software, assign a project manager, set a go-live date, and wonder why nothing transformative happens.

AI isn't a software implementation. It's a fundamental shift in how work gets done. It requires new skills, new processes, and new ways of approaching problems. The organizations that succeed treat AI adoption like learning a new language rather than installing a new printer.

Billion-dollar companies have stumbled because they try to boil the ocean by launching dozens of AI pilots simultaneously without building the foundation to support them. I have also seen small companies achieve remarkable results by focusing on one problem, solving it well, and building from there.

The key takeaway is that AI adoption is more about organizational change than technological deployment. The companies that remember this tend to succeed. The ones that don't become cautionary tales.

SECTION 1: AI ADOPTION FRAMEWORK

When it comes to AI adoption, the industry you are in matters. Not because AI itself behaves differently from sector to sector but because constraints, timelines, and success metrics can vary significantly.

In this section, we focus on a few industries where AI is already making a significant impact. While some of the frameworks we discuss here apply broadly, it's not intended to be a comprehensive overview of every sector. For a deeper dive into identifying high-impact AI use cases, refer back to Chapter 3, where we explored how to pinpoint the opportunities that matter most for your organization.

1.1 HEALTHCARE AND LIFE SCIENCES: THE REGULATION TANGO

If you are in healthcare, you already know that "move fast and break things" isn't exactly your motto. The FDA doesn't care that your AI model works 99% of the time. They want to know what happens with that remaining 1%!

I worked with a radiology group that spent a whole *two years* getting their AI diagnostic tool approved. But here is what they learned: the slow, methodical approach didn't just satisfy regulators, it built trust with doctors who were initially skeptical. By the time they launched, radiologists were actually asking to work with the AI assistant because they'd been involved in the development process.

The journey of healthcare AI typically unfolds in predictable stages. You start with administrative tasks such as scheduling, basic triage, or documentation. These applications are low-risk but high-impact, and they let you build internal expertise without touching patient care directly.

Next comes diagnostic support. This is where things get more complicated. Your AI system can flag potential issues, suggest additional tests, or highlight areas for closer examination. But it never makes the final call—this still stays with the physician.

The advanced phase involves predictive analytics and personalized treatment recommendations. This is where AI starts to shine, but it's also where regulatory complexity reaches its peak. Full integration takes three to five years minimum, assuming you have been building data infrastructure and expertise all along.

1.2 FINANCIAL SERVICES: TRUST BUT VERIFY

Banking moves faster than healthcare, but not by much. The difference is that financial institutions have been using algorithms for decades, including credit scoring, fraud detection, and risk management. AI is often an evolution of existing capabilities rather than a revolution.

The catch is that financial AI lives in a fishbowl. Every decision is scrutinized by regulators, audited by compliance teams, and questioned by customers. Your AI needs to be not just accurate but explainable. "The algorithm said so" doesn't fly when you are denying someone a loan.

Banks typically start with customer service chatbots and fraud detection enhancements. These applications provide immediate value while letting you work out the kinks in your AI governance processes. The timeline here is usually 12–18 months from pilot to full deployment.

The intermediate phase focuses on risk assessment and algorithmic trading improvements. This is when regulatory scrutiny intensifies. You need audit trails, bias testing, and fail-safes that satisfy both internal risk management and external regulators.

The advanced phase is where banks separate themselves from their competitors. Here, AI transforms core business operations through personalized wealth management, dynamic pricing models, and predictive analytics that can anticipate market shifts weeks in advance. Banks use AI to optimize their entire loan portfolio in real time, adjusting interest rates and credit limits based on constantly evolving risk profiles and market conditions.

This is also where AI starts making strategic decisions, such as identifying new market opportunities, predicting customer lifestyle changes, and even suggesting merger and acquisition targets. Technology becomes deeply embedded in the business strategy rather than just being used for operational efficiency. At this level, banks see AI contributing increasingly to their annual revenue growth.

However, the advanced phase requires sophisticated AI governance frameworks that most banks aren't prepared for. You need AI systems that can explain not just individual decisions but entire strategic recommendations. Regulatory requirements become a lot more complex when AI is impacting capital allocation and business direction. Success here depends as much on organizational readiness as technological capability.

1.3 MANUFACTURING AND SUPPLY CHAIN: IF IT AIN'T BROKE, DON'T FIX IT (BUT MAYBE IMPROVE IT)

Manufacturing companies often have the opposite problem. They are so focused on not ruining existing processes that they are afraid to try anything new. Once they start, however, they often see results faster than other industries.

The AI journey of a manufacturing company usually begins with predictive maintenance. You are not changing how things work, you are just getting better at predicting when they will break down. Return on investment (ROI) is immediate and measurable: less downtime, lower maintenance costs, and happier operators.

Quality control comes next. This includes computer vision systems that can spot defects humans might miss or catch them earlier in the process. These systems often pay for themselves within months through reduced waste and inefficiencies.

The advanced phase involves comprehensive supply chain optimization and autonomous production processes. This is where manufacturing AI gets truly transformative, but it also requires the most organizational change. It may take several years for full implementation, but the competitive advantages you gain are immeasurable.

1.4 RETAIL AND E-COMMERCE: THE SPEED OF CUSTOMER EXPECTATIONS

Retail moves at the speed of customer expectations, which means *fast*. Customers don't care about your AI implementation timeline; they want personalized experiences, accurate recommendations, and instant service as soon as possible.

The good news is that retail AI can often be deployed quickly. Recommendation engines, dynamic pricing, and chatbots can be up and running in weeks rather than months. The bad news is that customer expectations keep rising, so you are constantly chasing a moving target.

Retail AI typically starts with personalization, showing customers products they are likely to want based on their browsing and purchase history. The technology is mature, the ROI is clear, and the risk is relatively low.

The next phase involves inventory optimization and demand forecasting. This is less visible to customers but often more valuable to the business. Getting inventory right can make the difference between profit and loss, especially in thin-margin businesses.

Advanced retail AI includes comprehensive customer journey optimization and predictive analytics for trend identification. This is where retail AI becomes truly strategic, helping companies stay ahead of changing customer preferences and market trends.

1.5 PROFESSIONAL SERVICES: WHEN YOUR BRAIN IS YOUR BUSINESS

Here is the uncomfortable truth about professional services: when your entire business model is built on human expertise, AI feels like an existential threat. I get it. When you have spent decades building your reputation on knowing things other people don't, the idea of a machine doing that work faster and cheaper is terrifying.

Here is what I have learned from working with law firms, consulting companies, and accounting practices over the past few years: those that are thriving aren't the ones that ignored AI or that panicked because of it. They are the ones that figured out how to make AI make them better at being human.

In a law firm I worked with recently, the partners were convinced that AI would replace their junior associates. Instead, they discovered that AI could handle the mind-numbing contract review work that nobody looked forward to doing, freeing up their people to focus on the strategic thinking and fostering of client relationships that truly differentiated their firm. Their junior associates went from being glorified document processors to being strategic advisors. You can probably guess which version of the job was ultimately more satisfying.

AI in professional services usually starts with the essential yet tedious tasks, rather than going straight into the high-stakes work. This includes document analysis, basic research, and routine report generation. AI is perfect for this type of work. It doesn't get tired, it doesn't miss details, and it doesn't bill by the hour to read through standard lease agreements.

Legal firms are finding that AI can scan thousands of contracts in minutes, flagging unusual clauses and potential issues that would take associates hours or even days to identify.[1] Consulting firms are using AI to crunch through market data and generate initial insights, giving their consultants a head start on the analysis, which is the part that clients actually pay for.

The intermediate phase is where things get interesting. You start building client intelligence platforms that know more about your clients than they themselves know. What started out as an AI system for reading contracts has now expanded to analyzing all your client interactions, identifying patterns in their business challenges, and suggesting services before they even realize they need them.

This is where professional services AI becomes genuinely valuable rather than just efficient. You are not just faster, you are smarter too. You can spot opportunities that human analysis might miss, identify risks that aren't obvious, and provide insights that feel almost psychic to clients who are used to service providers that only know what they are explicitly told.

The advanced phase is where you stop just using AI to do existing work better and begin to use it to carry out tasks that were previously impossible. Predictive analytics that can forecast client needs months in advance. Automated report generation that creates customized deliverables for each client. AI-assisted strategic planning that can model scenarios and outcomes in real time during client meetings.

But here is the thing that most firms miss: the partners who are most successful with AI aren't the ones who let the machines make the decisions. They are the ones who use AI to gather information, identify patterns, and generate options faster than ever before, after which they apply their experience and wisdom to make the final calls.

The client doesn't want to pay for AI analysis. They want to pay for your interpretation of that analysis, your recommendations based on that interpretation, and your guidance on how to implement those recommendations. AI simply makes you better at providing that value—you are not meant to be redundant to it.

1.6 WHY SIZE MATTERS: THE SCALE ADVANTAGE AND DISADVANTAGE

The size of your organization plays a big role in how you approach AI. It affects everything from the resources you have to work with to how complex implementation will be. Whether you are a startup or a global enterprise, there will be benefits and hurdles along the way that impact the best path forward.

Large Enterprises: The Blessing and Curse of Resources

Large organizations have massive datasets, substantial budgets, dedicated teams, and the ability to absorb failures, unlike their smaller counterparts. Despite that, they also have potentially crippling disadvantages such as bureaucracy, legacy systems, organizational inertia, and the inability to move quickly.

If you are running AI initiatives in a large enterprise, your biggest enemy is complexity. You have multiple stakeholders with different priorities, systems that aren't designed to interact with each other, and processes that have been optimized for the pre-AI world that are stuck there.

The key is to start small but think big. Pick pilot projects that can succeed independently but also lay groundwork for broader transformation. A successful chatbot deployment might seem minor, but it can teach you about data integration, user acceptance, and change management that will be crucial for larger initiatives down the road.

Enterprise AI adoption typically follows a three-phase pattern. The foundation phase (months 1–6) is all about governance, data infrastructure, and pilot selection. This process feels slow, but skipping it leads to massive organizational problems down the road.

The scaling phase (months 7–18) is where things get interesting. You are rolling out successful pilots, integrating with existing systems, and dealing with the reality of organizational change. This is where most enterprises either find their stride or get bogged down in complexity.

The transformation phase (month 19+) is where AI becomes a fundamental part of how the organization operates. Cross-functional AI workflows, advanced analytics, and innovation labs become standard operating procedure. Getting here requires sustained commitment and excellent execution throughout the earlier phases.

Mid-Size Organizations: The Sweet Spot

Companies in this category have the best of both worlds. They have enough resources to manage AI seriously and enough agility to implement systems quickly. They can make decisions without committee approval, pivot when something isn't working, and scale successful initiatives rapidly.

The challenge they have is that mid-size companies often lack specialized knowledge. They don't have dedicated AI teams or unlimited consulting budgets. They need to build capabilities while implementing solutions, which can be overwhelming.

Success for medium-sized enterprises starts with quick wins. Off-the-shelf solutions that can deliver value immediately, such as customer service tools, basic analytics platforms, and productivity software are good choices. These wins build confidence and provide valuable learning opportunities.

The strategic integration phase focuses on custom solutions tailored to specific business needs. This is where mid-size companies can differentiate themselves from larger competitors by being more nimble and customer-focused.

The competitive advantage phase is where successful mid-size companies often outperform larger rivals. At this stage, they have built AI capabilities that are perfectly suited to their market niche, and they can adapt and improve faster than bigger organizations.

Small Companies: David's AI Slingshot[2]

Small organizations face resource constraints that seem insurmountable, but they also have advantages that shouldn't be underestimated. They can change direction overnight, adopt new tools instantly, and focus their limited resources on applications that deliver the most impact.

The key for small companies is to think AI-first rather than AI-later. Instead of trying to retrofit AI into existing processes, they can build new processes around AI capabilities. This often leads to more elegant and effective solutions than what larger organizations are capable of achieving.

Small company AI adoption typically starts with productivity tools such as AI-powered scheduling and basic CRM systems. These tools don't require major process changes, but they can dramatically increase efficiency.

The operational excellence phase focuses on customer experience improvements. Small companies can often provide personalized service that rivals much larger competitors by leveraging AI to analyze customer data and predict needs.

The growth acceleration phase is where AI becomes truly strategic for small companies. AI-powered market analysis, automated operations, and intelligent customer acquisition can enable growth that would otherwise require much larger teams.

1.7 THE READINESS REALITY CHECK

Before you start planning your AI journey, you need to run an honest assessment of where you stand. This isn't about being perfect, it's about being realistic.

Technical Readiness: The Foundation

Your data is probably messier than you think. I have worked with companies that thought they had great data until they tried to feed it to an AI system. Suddenly, they discovered inconsistent formats, missing fields, and quality issues that had been hidden in traditional reporting.

The data quality assessment should be brutal. Score yourself on a 1–10 scale, where ten means your data is AI-ready out of the box, and one means you are not even sure where all your data lives. Most organizations score between four and six, which means a significant amount of work needs to be done before serious AI implementation is considered.

Your IT infrastructure probably needs work too. AI systems are hungry. They consume computing resources, storage, and network bandwidth at unprecedented rates. Cloud readiness becomes crucial because AI workloads are often data-intensive and require scalable computing power. IT teams need to be ready for any surprises thrown their way.

Integration capabilities matter more than you might expect. AI systems need to share data with existing applications, trigger actions in current business systems, and provide insights where people actually work. If your systems don't talk to each other, your AI initiatives will struggle.

Organizational Readiness: The Human Factor

Leadership commitment isn't just about allocating budget, patience is a key factor as well. AI initiatives rarely deliver immediate, dramatic results. They require sustained investment, experimentation, and willingness to learn. Leaders who expect AI to solve all their problems quickly are setting themselves up for disappointment.

As AI changes how people work, change management capabilities become crucial. Employees need training not only in operating new tools but also in adopting entirely new approaches to their work. Organizations that can properly apply these principles hold a clear advantage.

Employee digital literacy varies more than most leaders realize. Your marketing team might be incredibly sophisticated with social media tools but struggle with data analysis software. Your operations team might be great with manufacturing systems but uncomfortable with AI interfaces.

Budget flexibility matters as well, because AI projects often don't follow traditional project patterns. You might need to pivot, scale up successful pilots quickly, or abandon initiatives that aren't delivering desired results. Traditional IT budgeting processes can become obstacles to AI success.

Cultural Readiness: The Determining Player

Having an innovative mindset isn't just about being open to new ideas but also being comfortable with uncertainty. AI implementation involves a lot of experimentation, and not all experiments succeed. Organizations that punish failure or require detailed ROI projections for every initiative will struggle.

Failure tolerance becomes especially important in AI projects because machine learning involves iterative improvement. Your first model will not be your best model. Organizations need to be comfortable with this evolutionary approach.

An emphasis on continuous learning becomes crucial as AI technology evolves rapidly. What works today might be obsolete in six months. Organizations that don't invest in ongoing education and skill development will find their AI capabilities quickly becoming outdated.

It's important to be open to external partnerships as no organization will have all the necessary skills to build AI capabilities internally. The most successful AI implementations often involve partnerships with vendors, consultants, research institutes, and even competitors. Organizations that try to go it alone often limit their potential.

SECTION 2: YOUR CAREER IN THE AI WORLD

Let's talk about something that keeps most professionals awake at night: whether or not AI will make your job obsolete. The short answer is probably not. The longer answer is that your job will likely change significantly, and the skills that made you successful in the past might not be enough for the future.

I have watched this transformation play out across dozens of organizations and impact hundreds of professionals. The people who thrive aren't necessarily the most technical. Often, they are the ones who learn to work *with* AI rather than against it or in spite of it.

2.1 THE NEW BASIC SKILLS

AI Literacy: Not Coding but Understanding

You don't need to become a data scientist, but you do need to understand how AI systems work well enough to use them effectively. This is like learning how to drive: you don't need to understand how internal engines work, but you need to know how to operate the controls safely.

AI fundamentals involve understanding what machine learning can and can't do. AI excels at pattern recognition, prediction, and optimization. It struggles with reasoning, causal inference, and handling novel situations. Knowing these strengths and limitations helps you apply AI appropriately.

Understanding AI capabilities means knowing when to trust AI outputs and when to be skeptical. If an AI system tells you something that seems too good to be true or that completely contradicts your domain expertise, it probably deserves closer scrutiny. AI systems can be confidently wrong, which is why human judgment remains crucial.

Ethical AI principles matter because AI systems can perpetuate and amplify human biases. If you are using AI to screen job candidates, evaluate loan applications, or make medical recommendations, you need to understand how bias can creep in, and what safeguard strategies are necessary.

Data privacy considerations become crucial as AI systems process more personal information. Understanding how to safely share data within AI systems, how to anonymize sensitive information, and what privacy regulations apply to your use cases, protects both you and your organization.

Prompt Engineering: The New Communication Skill

Prompt engineering is about learning to give clear instructions to AI systems in order to achieve desired results.[3] AI is like your very capable assistant, but one that takes everything literally. Thus, it is important that you phrase and structure your requests appropriately to ensure high-quality outputs.

Be specific about what you want when communicating with AI systems. Instead of saying "analyze this data," you might ask to "identify the top three factors that correlate with customer churn in this dataset, and explain why each factor might be causally related to churn."

Context management becomes critical when working on complex projects. AI systems don't always remember previous conversations or understand implied context. It's important to learn how to provide appropriate background information and maintain context across multiple interactions to dramatically improve results.

Output optimization involves understanding how to refine and improve AI-generated content. This might mean providing feedback on writing style, asking for alternative approaches to problems, or combining outputs from multiple AI iterations into coherent final products.

Multi-model interaction skills are becoming increasingly important as AI systems handle text, images, audio, and video. Your AI communication will be significantly more effective if you know when to use visual inputs instead of text descriptions, or when audio outputs might be more useful than written summaries.

Data Fluency: The New Numeracy

You don't need to become a statistician, but you do need enough statistical literacy to interpret AI outputs correctly. Go out of your way to gain a basic statistical understanding of concepts including correlation versus causation, statistical significance, and confidence intervals. These concepts help you analyze AI-generated insights and avoid drawing incorrect conclusions from data analysis.

Data interpretation skills help you extract meaningful conclusions from AI-generated reports and visualizations. This includes understanding different types of charts and graphs, recognizing trends and patterns in data, and translating data insights into actionable business recommendations.

Quality assessment abilities help you assess whether data sources and AI analyses are reliable and relevant. This includes recognizing biased or incomplete data and understanding how sample size affects reliability. It is also important to know when additional data collection might be necessary.

Understanding data visualization is becoming more and more important as AI systems generate increasingly sophisticated charts, graphs, and interactive displays. Being able to quickly understand and interpret these visualizations helps you extract insights and communicate findings to others efficiently.

2.2 ROLE-SPECIFIC EVOLUTION

Executive Leadership: Strategy in the AI Age

Executive leadership should approach AI from a strategic perspective, not a technical one. Your focus must be on the broader implications to your organization. For example, how AI can create a sustainable competitive edge, generate new revenue streams, and fundamentally reshape your business model to stay competitive and continuously grow. Deciding which specific tool to use in different scenarios is an operational matter that follows strategic direction.

Proper AI governance becomes crucial as AI systems make decisions that impact customers, employees, and business outcomes. You need frameworks for ensuring AI systems operate ethically, transparently, and in alignment with organizational values. This includes understanding regulatory requirements and making sure your company's image is always protected.

Effective leaders must also master investment prioritization, a critical discipline for AI success. Investment prioritization involves strategically allocating resources by evaluating which AI initiatives offer the greatest potential, align best with core business goals, and have the most feasible timelines. Knowing where your assets are most valuable will help streamline company operations and increase likelihood that projects are successfully executed.

Middle Management: The AI Translation Layer

Middle managers face unique challenges in AI adoption because they must connect executive vision with day-to-day operations. This means that this role serves a dual responsibility: interpreting strategy and driving execution. You must understand the executive plan for AI, and guide your teams to turn that plan into operational reality.

Managing AI projects is vastly different from traditional project management. AI initiatives are experimental by nature, so you are often testing ideas without knowing if they will actually succeed. These projects depend heavily on data quality and availability, and they develop through cycles of testing and refinement rather than following linear timelines. Conventional project management playbooks will need significant modification to be effective for this iterative process and its inherent uncertainty.

The job of coordinating diverse teams also becomes more complex, as AI projects often need to bring IT, business operations, data analysts, and external vendors together to achieve their goals. Your job is to help these team members communicate effectively despite their varying levels of technical knowledge. You need to ensure that what is technically possible coincides with what the business actually needs.

Perhaps the most complex task you will face is integrating AI into existing workflows. This involves understanding what the impact of AI is on current processes. Based on that understanding, build training programs to help your team learn to work with these new tools. You also need to carefully observe and manage the change to ensure productivity remains high. Navigating this successfully requires a combination of technical understanding and strong people management.

Success also needs to be measured differently. You will require new metrics, as traditional ones often fail to capture its true value. You will also need to set new indicators that reflect both desired operational improvements and strategic goals, and then effectively communicate this new framework to your team.

Individual Contributors: Augmentation, Not Replacement

If you are an individual contributor, your focus should be on becoming more effective through AI collaboration. The most successful professionals learn to use AI's strengths, while simultaneously maintaining their unique human capabilities.

Domain-specific AI applications represent the most immediately valuable skills. A marketing professional might focus on AI tools for content creation and campaign optimization, while a financial analyst might emphasize AI-powered forecasting and risk assessment tools. The key is developing expertise surrounding AI applications that enhance your core competencies.

Quality control and data validation skills are more important than ever before, as AI outputs need to be checked for accuracy and suitability. You must learn to assess how reliable AI-generated content is, verify its insights, and determine when human review is needed. This judgment is one of your most valuable skills in AI-enhanced work.

Creative problem-solving will become your competitive edge. As AI takes over routine analysis and data processing, your ability to think creatively becomes more valuable than ever. The skills that will set you apart include approaching problems from new angles, spotting connections that others miss, and developing innovative solutions. While AI can analyze patterns and process information quickly, humans excel at reframing challenges and thinking outside the constraints of established frameworks.

Effective communication is more critical than ever when working on AI projects. Your role will involve clearly explaining AI-driven insights to your colleagues, collaborating with people of varying technical expertise, and ensuring that the capabilities of AI are aligned with practical business objectives.

This means your role will be critical for translating between the technical and the practical. You may need to clarify an AI recommendation to a coworker or explain to stakeholders about what the technology can or cannot do. You may even need to manage workflows that mix automated work with human tasks. Your ability to manage these scenarios is a fundamental requirement for success.

2.3 THE CONTINUOUS LEARNING FRAMEWORK

The half-life of AI skills is getting shorter. What you learn today might be obsolete in a few years. This is a typical feature of rapid technological progress. The key is developing learning strategies that keep pace with the rate of change.

Personal Development Framework

Regular skill assessment will help you understand how your skills align with changing requirements. The goal is to identify which AI competencies are essential in your field right now so you can narrow down the specific gaps you should address. Keep in mind that comparing your skills to AI experts is not always helpful, unless your role requires those skills.

Given the amount of AI information out there, it is important to select your learning resources very carefully. Focus on information from reputable sources. A good way to learn is to balance theory with hands-on practice. You should follow a structured path to build a complete skill set; simply accumulating isolated information is not as helpful.

Keep looking for opportunities to practice. This is essential because AI skills are learned through use rather than study. Look for chances to apply AI tools in your current work, volunteer for AI-related projects, and experiment with new AI applications in low-risk situations.

Building a network with other professionals navigating similar AI transitions provides you with support, learning opportunities, and career intelligence. To stay current, actively engage with the AI professional community. For example, you can join industry-specific AI groups, attend relevant conferences, and participate in online forums where practitioners exchange real-world insights. I also want to point out that AI development is international in nature, so it's important to expand your view beyond your immediate surroundings.

Career Transition Planning

Career planning in the AI era starts with understanding how your current job might evolve as technology advances. Prepare yourself for a complete transformation, as most positions will be enhanced by AI, even if it hasn't happened to your industry yet. That being said, most positions will be enhanced by AI, not replaced, at least in the immediate future.

So this mindset shift is not to prepare for unemployment but to strategically position yourself for the significant changes that are happening.

Create a list of your current abilities to see which ones will remain valuable as AI becomes more widespread. Skills like creative problem-solving, building relationships, and strategic thinking typically become more important over time. Concurrently, routine tasks such as basic data analysis or standard reporting may become less valuable, as AI handles these functions more efficiently and accurately.

AI is also creating entirely new types of jobs and career opportunities. This might include roles like AI trainers who teach systems to work better, specialists who help teams collaborate effectively with AI tools, or positions that combine your existing expertise with AI knowledge. Be aware of these emerging opportunities, as they can help you position yourself for future growth.

The key to having a successful career alongside AI is to have a clear mind first. You are already ahead of others if you can clearly understand and communicate what you bring to the table that technology cannot. This means identifying how you add value beyond what AI systems can provide and being able to explain that value to your employer and colleagues. Your unique combination of experience, judgment, and human insight becomes your strongest asset in an AI-enhanced workplace.

SECTION 3: MEASURING WHAT ACTUALLY MATTERS

Here is where most organizations get AI measurement completely wrong: they focus on traditional ROI calculations, while missing the transformative impacts that make AI truly valuable. This is like measuring the internet's success by how much it reduces paper usage, which may be technically accurate but completely misses the point. We discussed AI project ROI calculation in detail in Chapter 3. In this section, we will briefly recap on its implications and point out additional aspects organizations should consider.

3.1 THE ROI TRAP

Measuring AI's ROI requires a non-traditional approach. Unlike predictable technologies with clear cost benefits, AI's value often emerges gradually as organizations learn, adapt, and integrate it into core processes. Its flexibility makes it difficult to quantify financially.

I have seen organizations abandon promising AI initiatives because they didn't demonstrate clear ROI within the six-month timeframe they set. I have also seen companies achieve massive competitive advantages from AI investments that initially looked questionable on spreadsheets. The difference usually comes down to their measurement approach.

That being said, traditional financial metrics such as cost reduction, revenue growth, and efficiency gains are still important. The problem is that they only provide a partial view of the total value AI creates, overlooking AI's broader strategic impact.

AI's most significant benefits, such as expanding market share through innovation, increasing customer loyalty via enhanced service, and strengthening your competitive position with unique capabilities, are often achieved in the long term and will take time to show up in the balance sheets. These are the factors that will help your organization create long-lasting advantages.

The key is to balance short-term financial metrics with longer-term strategic indicators. You need enough immediate and measurable returns to justify continued investment, but you also need to measure progress toward transformative capabilities that create a lasting competitive advantage.

3.2 OPERATIONAL EXCELLENCE: THE HIDDEN MULTIPLIER

Operational improvements from AI often provide the foundation for financial returns, rather than generating immediate revenue. Process optimization, quality improvements, and efficiency gains create capabilities that enable future growth and profitability.

Shortening product development cycles might not show immediate profit but creates significant value by allowing the company to respond more quickly to market changes and launch new products faster. Error rate reduction in manufacturing processes may show modest immediate savings but builds a reputation for quality that drives long-term customer loyalty. These improvements often compound over time, creating competitive advantages that become increasingly difficult for rivals to match.

3.3 HUMAN-FOCUSED METRICS: THE ULTIMATE MEASURE OF SUCCESS

The long-term success of AI often depends on the impact it has on employees. Systems that boost job satisfaction, foster skill development, and open paths for advancement are more sustainable than those focused solely on automation.

Job satisfaction improvements might result from AI handling routine tasks and enabling employees to focus on more engaging, creative, and strategic work. Skill development acceleration might occur as AI tools enable employees to take on more sophisticated responsibilities and learn new capabilities.

Customer experience excellence represents another crucial dimension, as AI's customer-facing impacts often determine long-term success. Satisfaction improvements, service quality enhancements, personalization effectiveness, and response time optimization all contribute to customer loyalty and word-of-mouth marketing.

The human-centric perspective recognizes that AI success ultimately depends on human acceptance and adoption. Technologies that create negative experiences for employees or customers will struggle to achieve lasting success, regardless of their technical sophistication.

3.4 COMPETITIVE POSITIONING

The biggest benefit of AI lies in its ability to improve long-term competitiveness, not immediate ROI. For example, AI can deliver highly personalized customer experiences that improve loyalty and differentiate your brand. This capability also creates a significant barrier to entry, as competitors would need to invest heavily to develop similar systems. Over time, these advantages compound, strengthening your market position and making it more defensible.

Brand reputation improvements from innovative AI applications or superior AI-powered customer service create intangible value that is difficult to quantify but is extremely valuable. Organizations known for AI excellence often enjoy customer acquisition advantages and premium pricing opportunities.

Innovation acceleration through AI capabilities enables organizations to develop new products, services, and business models more quickly than competitors. This innovation capability becomes increasingly valuable in rapidly changing markets, where the competitive advantage goes to organizations that can adapt and innovate quickly.

Intellectual property creation through AI implementations provides a tangible measure of innovation value. Patents, trade secrets, and proprietary algorithms developed through AI initiatives create assets that can generate revenue through licensing and can provide competitive protection.

3.5 RISK MITIGATION

AI-powered predictive analytics and automated monitoring systems significantly increase risk mitigation effectiveness. This helps organizations avoid costly problems and respond more quickly to emerging threats.

These capabilities become especially valuable in complex, regulated industries where compliance failures can be extremely expensive.

For example, it is extremely important to have AI systems that can maintain functionality during disruptions. Such improvements to operational continuity become especially valuable during crisis situations when human-dependent processes might be compromised.

3.6 IMPLEMENTATION: MAKING MEASUREMENT WORK

Dashboard Design

Effective AI measurement requires balanced scorecards that include financial, operational, customer, and learning perspectives. The balanced mix of leading and lagging indicators ensures a comprehensive understanding of AI impact across different timeframes and stakeholder groups.

Stakeholder-specific metrics ensure that different audiences receive information relevant to their roles and responsibilities. Executive dashboards emphasize strategic and financial indicators, operational managers focus on process improvements, and customer-facing teams prioritize experience metrics.

Real-time monitoring capabilities enable rapid response to performance changes and emerging opportunities. Automated reporting reduces administrative burden while ensuring consistent information distribution. Exception alerts highlight situations requiring immediate attention.

Trend analysis capabilities help identify patterns and predict future performance. These tools become especially important for AI implementations because benefits often emerge gradually and may not be obvious in point-in-time measurements.

Continuous Improvement

Performance review cycles provide systematic evaluation opportunities that help organizations learn from both successes and failures. Regular assessment schedules ensure consistent attention to measurement and improvement opportunities.

Benchmark comparisons help organizations understand their performance relative to industry standards and best practices. These comparisons become especially valuable as standard AI adoption measures and industry benchmarks become more established.

Goal adjustment mechanisms enable organizations to modify targets as they gain experience and a better understanding of AI capabilities. This flexibility is important as AI potential often exceeds initial expectations, and companies need to adjust their ambitions accordingly.

Learning integration processes ensures that AI measurement insights contribute to organizational knowledge and future planning. This includes documenting lessons learned, sharing best practices, and incorporating conclusions drawn from performance metrics into strategic planning processes.

SECTION 4: YOUR FIRST STEPS—MAKING IT REAL

After working with dozens of organizations on their AI journeys, I have learned that the difference between success and failure usually comes down to how well they handle the first 90 days. Get those right, and you build momentum that carries through the entire transformation. Get them wrong, and you will end up fighting uphill battles for months or even years to come.

4.1 WEEKS 1–4: THE FOUNDATION PHASE

The Honest Assessment

Your first task is to be brutally honest about self-assessment. Not the kind where you tell yourself what you want to hear, but the kind where you acknowledge the uncomfortable truth about your current capabilities and constraints.

Start with your data. Don't assume it's AI-ready just because it works fine for generating standard reports. AI systems are pickier than traditional analytics; they need consistent formatting, exhaustive records, and clean integration between different data sources. Spend time actually looking at your data, not just reading reports about it.

Assess your technical infrastructure realistically. Can your current systems handle the computing requirements of AI workloads? Do you have the network bandwidth for data-intensive applications? Can your existing software integrate with AI platforms? Overlooking these factors can kill promising initiatives.

Evaluate your readiness honestly. Ask questions like, "do you have leaders that are committed to sustained investment even when results aren't immediately obvious?" "Do you have change management capabilities that can help employees adapt to new ways of working?" "Do you have the budget flexibility to pivot when initial approaches don't work?"

Identifying Your Starting Point

Don't try to boil the ocean. Pick one or two use cases that can provide learning opportunities while delivering meaningful value for your business. The best initial AI projects share several key characteristics: they solve real problems, they don't require extensive integration with existing systems, they have clear success metrics, and they can be implemented reasonably quickly.

Customer service enhancement often makes a good starting point because the impact is immediately visible, the technology is mature, and the risk is relatively low. Process automation provides another good entry point, especially for organizations with repetitive, rule-based tasks that consume a significant amount of employees' time.

Avoid the temptation to start with the most complex or strategically important applications. Save those for when you have built experience and confidence. Your first AI project should be a learning experience that builds organizational capabilities, paving the way for more high-stakes initiatives later on.

Building Your Team

AI initiatives require diverse expertise that most organizations don't have in-house. You need technical proficiency, business knowledge, project management skills, and change management capabilities, among others. You likely won't be able to hire employees with all these skills immediately, so focus on building a team that can learn together.

Look for people who are curious about AI, rather than experts. The field is evolving so quickly that yesterday's expertise might be obsolete tomorrow. What matters more is the ability to learn quickly, adapt to changing requirements, and collaborate effectively across different disciplines. In the words of Shunryu Suzuki, "In the beginner's mind there are many possibilities, in the expert's there are few."[4]

Don't forget about change management. AI initiatives succeed or fail based on human adoption as much as technical implementation. Having someone who understands how to help people adapt to new ways of working can make all the difference.

Consider external partnerships for specialized expertise. AI consultants, system integrators, and technology vendors can provide capabilities that you don't have internally. The key is structuring these partnerships to build internal capabilities rather than create dependencies.

4.2 MONTHS 1–6: BUILDING MOMENTUM

Pilot Project Execution

When planning your AI pilot project, make learning your primary objective, rather than simply demonstrating that the technology works. Design your pilot to uncover important insights surrounding what data you need, how the system will integrate with existing processes, how people will actually use it, and what organizational changes will be required for success.

Be upfront with stakeholders that AI systems rarely work perfectly on the first try. These technologies need time to improve through testing, adjustments, and continuous fine-tuning. Make sure your project timeline and communication plan account for this reality. When stakeholders understand that iteration is a normal part of AI development, they are more likely to stay supportive when the initial results aren't perfect.

Document everything. What works, what doesn't, what surprises you, what you wish you'd known earlier. This documentation becomes invaluable as you scale successful approaches and avoid repeating past mistakes.

Measure impact carefully. Don't just focus on whether the AI system works technically; measure its impact on business processes, employee satisfaction, and customer experience. These broader impacts often determine long-term success more than technical performance.

Skill Development

AI literacy shouldn't be limited to your technical specialists. While different roles need different levels of expertise, everyone in your organization needs a basic understanding of how AI works and how it will change their day-to-day responsibilities. This foundation helps people adapt more quickly and reduces resistance to new AI tools.

Emphasize practical skills over technical theory. Teach people how to work productively with AI systems, understand and validate AI-generated results, and incorporate AI tools into their current work processes. Most employees don't need to understand the technical details, but they do need to know how to use AI effectively in their jobs.

Avoid a one-size-fits-all approach to training programs. It is way more effective to have targeted learning paths based on how different departments will actually use AI. For example, marketing teams need to understand AI applications for customer insights and content creation, and operations teams need to focus more on process optimization and quality control. Customized training is more relevant and practical for participants.

Governance Development

Establish governance frameworks early on, before you actually need them. It is much easier to set up ethical guidelines, risk management processes, and decision-making authority when you are working on small pilots, rather than when things have picked up and you are dealing with organization-wide implementations.

Focus on principles rather than detailed procedures. AI technology evolves too quickly for in-depth policies to remain relevant, but core principles concerning ethics, transparency, and accountability provide lasting guidance.

Include diverse perspectives in governance discussions. AI systems can impact customers, employees, and communities in ways that may not be obvious to technical teams. Having a diverse set of voices in these discussions helps identify potential issues before they become problems.

Build governance capabilities gradually. Start with basic guidelines for your pilot projects and expand them as you gain experience and begin to tackle more complex applications.

4.3 YEAR 1+: SUSTAINABLE TRANSFORMATION

Achieving Strategic Integration

At this stage, AI starts to fundamentally change how your organization works. Instead of running separate AI projects in different departments, you'll be building connected AI capabilities that work together across multiple business areas.

Develop AI platforms and shared infrastructure that can support multiple different applications. This approach makes future AI projects less expensive and less complex, while ensuring that all your AI systems work well together. Think of it as building the foundation that will support all your future AI initiatives.

Build internal AI expertise that can drive innovation, rather than merely implementing vendor solutions. This may involve hiring AI specialists, developing partnerships with research institutions, or creating internal innovation labs.

Create feedback loops that enable continuous improvement of AI capabilities. This includes monitoring AI performance, gathering user feedback, and incorporating lessons learned into future implementations.

Develop Organizational AI Capabilities

In today's competitive business environment, it is critical for organizations to develop internal AI skills to stay competitive. Organizations need teams that understand both the technical aspects of AI, and how it applies to business strategy. These skills help teams identify opportunities and translate complex AI concepts into practical business solutions.

Create comprehensive training programs that help current employees develop AI skills, while also attracting new AI talent to your organization. Provide clear career paths for AI professionals, establish mentorship programs, and build a culture of continuous learning that keeps up with the fast pace of AI innovation.

Invest in scalable AI infrastructure to support growing demands. This includes upgrading computational resources, developing efficient machine learning operations (MLOps) processes, and automating model maintenance. These steps help reduce the day-to-day operational load and ensure your AI initiatives run smoothly and effectively.

4.4 CREATE SUSTAINABLE COMPETITIVE ADVANTAGE

Focus on developing AI capabilities that your competitors can't easily copy. This means leveraging your unique data, creating specialized algorithms, and building AI-powered business models that are hard to replicate. The goal is to create sustainable advantages that become stronger over time, rather than temporary improvements that others can quickly match.

Look for ways to use AI to enable new products, services, or business models rather than just improving existing operations. These innovations often provide the most substantial long-term value from AI investments.

Build ecosystem partnerships that enhance your AI capabilities and market positioning. This includes partnerships with AI vendors, research institutions, or other organizations in your industry value chain.

Invest in research and development that positions your organization as an AI innovator in your industry. This means exploring cutting-edge technologies, conducting original research, and developing proprietary solutions that could become the foundation for future competitive advantages. Building a reputation for innovation attracts top talent, creates new business opportunities, and strengthens your market position.

Build Innovation Ecosystems

Your ecosystem should include technology providers, research institutions, and other organizations that complement your AI capabilities. These partnerships should go beyond basic vendor relationships to include joint research initiatives and ecosystem-wide innovation programs.

Establish external strategic development programs such as accelerators, venture funds, or partnership networks that give you early access to emerging AI technologies and startups. These programs can serve as early warning systems for disruptive technologies, while providing opportunities to invest in or acquire promising innovations.

Develop thought leadership positions that attract top talent, potential partners, and customer interest. Organizations recognized as AI innovators often enjoy preferential access to resources, partnerships, and market opportunities that further accelerate their competitive positioning in the AI-driven economy.

NOTES

1. Staff writer, "AI Contract Management: 80% Time Savings in Legal Work." *Virtasant*, 2025, virtasant.com/ai-today/ai-contract-mangement-legal.
2. "David's New Slingshot: How a Mid-Tier Trading Firm uses AI to Down Giants." *causaLens*, 2025, causalens.com/customer-stories/davids-new-slingshot-how-a-mid-tier-trading-firm-uses-ai-to-down-giants.
3. "Prompt Engineering: Overview and Guide." *Google Cloud*, cloud.google.com/discover/what-is-prompt-engineering.
4. Hartman, Zenkei Blanche. "The Zen of Not Knowing." *Tricycle: The Buddhist Review*, 2022, tricycle.org/article/zen-not-knowing/.

Conclusion

The Path Forward: Embracing the Journey

As this book comes to an end, remember that your artificial intelligence (AI) journey is only beginning. Real success comes from taking that first step, adapting as things change, and learning along the way. No one has it figured out from the start. Use the frameworks given here as a foundation, and let your organization's needs shape the path you take forward.

Transformation is made possible through technology, but it's not only about technology. It is also about how we apply these technologies to the work that we care about. This means that when we explore new possibilities, we need to stay grounded in our human values and drive progress responsibly. And that progress should deliver values for all people within society, rather than serving purely financial interests.

The next phase of AI in business will be led by people who can combine clear thinking, strong ethical values, and effective leadership. It will be those who stay curious during uncertain times and lead with purpose, not just ambition. The real question is whether we have what it takes to shape this transformation, or only react to it.

You don't need all the answers to get started. You just need to begin asking better questions, pay close attention to what you learn, and take that first deliberate step.

The future isn't something we wait for. It's something we build intentionally together.

DOI: 10.1201/9781003644699-11

Index

Note: *Italicized* page numbers indicate figures, while **bold** page numbers indicate tables.

B

E

F

G

N

O

P

Q

R

V

W

Z

For Product Safety Concerns and Information please contact our EU representative GPSR@taylorandfrancis.com
Taylor & Francis Verlag GmbH, Kaufingerstraße 24, 80331 München, Germany

www.ingramcontent.com/pod-product-compliance
Ingram Content Group UK Ltd.
Pitfield, Milton Keynes, MK11 3LW, UK
UKHW022129190926
475702UK00013B/1710

* 9 7 8 1 0 4 1 0 8 2 8 8 0 *